D0843102

RDED

Elizabeth Bishop: The Art of Travel

Elizabeth Bishop
The Art of Travel

Kim Fortuny

UNIVERSITY PRESS OF COLORADO

© 2003 by the University Press of Colorado

Published by the University Press of Colorado
5589 Arapahoe Avenue, Suite 206C
Boulder, Colorado 80303

All rights reserved
Printed in the United States of America

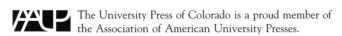 The University Press of Colorado is a proud member of
the Association of American University Presses.

The University Press of Colorado is a cooperative publishing enterprise supported, in part,
by Adams State College, Colorado State University, Fort Lewis College, Mesa State College,
Metropolitan State College of Denver, University of Colorado, University of Northern
Colorado, and Western State College of Colorado.

The paper used in this publication meets the minimum requirements of the American National Standard for Information Sciences—Permanence of Paper for Printed Library Materials. ANSI Z39.48-1992

Library of Congress Cataloging-in-Publication Data

Fortuny, Kim.
  Elizabeth Bishop : the art of travel / Kim Fortuny.
    p. cm.
  Includes bibliographical references (p.) and index.
  ISBN 0-87081-741-8 (alk. paper)
    1. Bishop, Elizabeth, 1911–1979—Criticism and interpretation. 2. Women and literature—
United States—History—20th century. 3. Bishop, Elizabeth, 1911–1979—Political and
social views. 4. Travelers in literature. 5. Travel in literature. I. Title.
  PS3503.I785Z666 2003
  811'.54—dc21
                                                                            2003008783

Design by Daniel Pratt

12 11 10 09 08 07 06 05 04 03   10 9 8 7 6 5 4 3 2 1

Kim Fortuny received her Ph.D. from the University of Iowa. She is presently an assistant
professor at Bogazici University in Istanbul, Turkey.

To Darlene Fortuny, mother and best friend

Contents

Foreword

BY DAVID HAMILTON

THE SOUL OF KIM FORTUNY'S STUDY is her extended treatment of three challenging and moderately lengthy poems, "Questions of Travel," "Over 2,000 Illustrations and a Complete Concordance," and "Crusoe in England." These fine poems, which are difficult to describe in any formal way, and of which there is as yet far from enough critical writing, "extend the personal into the realm of the poetic," to paraphrase Fortuny herself, a poetic always fraught with social-political awareness. For if Bishop was a traveler, which we all know, she traveled, too, along and within the lines of poetry in English, testing and extending them, tilting them toward prose, in these cases especially, as in others toward a blues song or a nursery rhyme. The negotiations of nuance and of just what, in her ear, "would suffice" to make a line, then another line and another, became the constructions of her few but prized collections. Yet at the same time, and at least equally, she traveled by constantly testing her awareness of her web of relation to the material world: places, houses, the people she found along the way: servants, employees, neighbors, shopkeepers, lovers, and friends. Again and again Bishop made herself aware of individuals, paid close attention to them, and would labor—since her poems often took years to complete—to portray them in lines as individual as the persons she knew and observed.

The material of the world demands prose for its close observation, Bishop would seem to say. Yet observation itself and the attention that requires, slightly heightened, confirmed and reconfirmed by steady, incremental revision, lead toward poetry, that is they lead toward the visionary realms of creative understanding and interpretation.

It may not take a traveler to read a traveler, but one can understand the affinity. Fortuny too thrives on travel. Turkey for her is the Brazil of Bishop, a country that extends and tests the margins of a North American consciousness, both socially and aesthetically. A country that places another language on the tongue and so reshapes the mind some as skill in the second language increases.

None of this may be necessary, but these experiences influence and inform the understandings of this book. "I knew nothing firsthand about

Brazil," Fortuny writes in an unpublished essay about her journey there. "Because her questions of travel have provided me with hard ways of think-ing about my own wanderings, I decided I should not write another sen-tence until I had laid my eyes and feet upon the country that had afforded Bishop the longest respite from her most debilitating cares, and a few of the better poems by a North American writer in the 20th century." If Bishop trusted in particulars, lifting them again and again into the realm of poetry and art, Fortuny wished to know some of those particulars for herself and to see what if any residue of Bishop's attention she might find in them.

And so she journeys by bus to Petrópolis, then by taxi, local auto, and foot to tinier and more remote Samambaia, following the hint of orchids—how often had Bishop mentioned orchids in her letters—to the high wooden gate of the house, no longer Bishop's and locked to Fortuny, that stands beneath the black cliffs from which Bishop's waterfalls hang:

> vapor
> climbs up the thick growth
> effortlessly, turns back
> holding them both,
> house and rock,
> in a private cloud.
>   "Song for the Rainy Season"

It is a cloud that Fortuny penetrates briefly and savors until a sudden storm drives her into a Bavarian teahouse across the way, from which she can still step out and look up to the black rock. "There was no mistake. It was weeping for joy."

Fortuny's travel was a kind of research, perhaps no more important than other more traditional research, but a serious grounding in her own subject matter. "I knew this landscape," Fortuny adds. "I'd been here two-hundred times." Traces of that confidence seem now to reside in Fortuny's own sentences. She writes cleanly and with graceful authority as she probes the mind and art of a poet beyond resolving, but one whose work survives to refresh our own travels, wherever we may venture today. Meanwhile, I have found no better guide to my own returns to the poetry of Elizabeth Bishop than these pages by another rare traveler, Kim Fortuny.

Acknowledgments

SPECIAL THANKS TO MY SISTER JILL FORTUNY, my father Jim Fortuny, and Isabelle Cooper for their friendship. I am also grateful to Richard Styles and the late Anita Styles for their example and encouragement. I particularly acknowledge Hélène and Gerard Gonsard, the Lombard-Breaux family, Ellen Cardin, Tom Lutz, Garrett Stewart, Ed Folsom, and my friends at Bosphorus University in Istanbul. I am grateful to David Hamilton for his long-distance support and intimate attention to the details of writing. And finally, great thanks to Bruno Gonsard from beginning to end.

In walking across these thick beds of mimosae, a broad track was marked by the change of shade, produced by the drooping of their sensitive petioles. It is easy to specify the individual objects of admiration in these grand scenes: but it is impossible to give an adequate idea of the higher feelings of wonder, astonishment, and devotion, which fill and elevate the mind.

—CHARLES DARWIN, THE VOYAGE OF THE BEAGLE

Introduction

With a philosophical flourish Cato throws himself upon his sword;
I quietly take to the ship.

—MELVILLE

I

THE FOLLOWING PROSE EXCERPT from a nearly linear, almost personal narrative offers a fine and wholly typical example of the political power of poetic interruption in a Bishop text. In "To the Botequim & Back" (1970), the speaker is walking to Joao Pica Pau's store in Ouro Prêto ("Black Gold"), Brazil, the Baroque mining town situated about 300 miles northwest of Rio de Janeiro where Bishop lived in the last of her "three loved houses." Built in the 1690s and restored by Bishop in the 1960s, the house remains in private hands; and the town since Bishop's death has been proclaimed a World Heritage Site by the United Nations Educational, Scientific, and Cultural Organization (UNESCO) thanks to the efforts of some of her former Brazilian friends and neighbors.[1] This patronage has resulted in the admirable restoration of much of Ouro Prêto's colonial architecture.

"Dona Elizabetchy," as she was known by locals, is remembered by only a few there today. No one, however, has forgotten the African slaves the Portuguese imported to mine the hills and build the European-style structures. Their descendants still live in—or, more often, on the outskirts of—

this beautifully preserved town where the poor continue their struggle for self-preservation within and beyond the classified limits of the city. These are some of the people Bishop directs us to consider in her short prose piece.

> Just before I get to João Pica Pau's, which is next to the barbershop, I meet three boys of twelve or so, brothers by their looks, all about the same size, mulattoes, with dark gray eyes. The two outside boys are helping the middle one, who is very thin, wasted, pale, wearing boots on his bare feet. He is languid and limp; his ragged shirt and blue trousers are very clean. He drags his feet and bends and sways like a broken stalk. His head turns toward me and he seems to have only one eye, a sunken hole for the other one—or is it an eye? I can't bear to look. (*Collected Prose* 75)

But of course she does, and what she sees stops the heart—then sets the mind kenning on the awful power in a routine gesture, on human dignity glanced through a barber's poor doors.

> His brother suddenly puts an arm under his knees and picks him up and takes him into the barber's. The barbershop is barely big enough for the chair, the barber, a fly-specked mirror, and an enormous atomizer. (At other times I've gone by, a child had been playing with the atomizer, spraying a rich synthetic scent out the door at his friends.) I glance in now and there are *two* people in the barber chair, the one-eyed boy sitting on his brother's lap, while the barber cuts his long frizzy hair. Everyone is silent as the brother holds him in a tight embrace. The boy cocks his one eye helplessly at the mirror. (*Collected Prose* 75)

There is no reaching after literary effect, yet the paragraph's final emotional thrust is powerful. There is no studied striving after a political message, yet the commentary is as implicitly social as the most earnest propaganda.

If we are moved, the means are hidden within the casual recesses of the prose. The drama builds slowly, almost indifferently. Tragic details are set alongside attractive or neutral ones: the boy is "wearing boots on his bare feet," but he is given the benefit of the Proustian adjective "languid"; his shirt is "ragged," his trousers are blue, and both are "very clean." And just as we emerge from a seemingly purposeless aside about an atomizer as arsenal, we are sideswiped, as it were, by the final drama in the chair, where "everyone is silent" as one brother holds another in the "tight embrace" of duty, familial protection, the love that saves us, the human triumph and despair this sudden gesture and noun phrase bring boiling to the surface of the paragraph.

Yet at the same time this isolated moment feels as natural to the landscape of the short prose piece as the maidenhair ferns and mosses that grow there. There is no trace of the tourist's mooning over exotic kinds of poverty. The scene and people are as real and present as they must be in the world and in an art in which the moments that shock us into a state of knowledge do so because room has already been made for them in our schemata. Bishop surprises us by not surprising us. She leads us to large understandings through sleights of language that bring us along before we realize we have left.

And this has important repercussions when considered in political terms—how reducing distances, geographical and intellectual, means engaging readers in lives that, although they are lived in the hills of Brazil, are surprisingly familiar or understandable and thus somehow necessary to our own. Although the boy "cocks his one eye helplessly at the mirror," Bishop does not patronize him. She allows him human vanity. And just as she sanctions gas stations in other poems to signify beyond their limited means, she makes modern man's complication with mirrors resonate down the narrow street as the speaker walks on. We are not forced to read the boy in the mirror as a reversed reflection of another, happier, wealthier image of himself. Degradation is not so simple, not so binarily disposed to haves or have-nots. If we like, however, we can consider the strength in that one eye. It may be "helpless," but it is nevertheless "cocked," thus very much alive. It is because of lines like these that Bishop continues to attract readers into the twenty-first century.

II

Bishop once said that San Francisco's literary and social scene in the late 1960s made her feel "either awfully old-fashioned or rather new" (*One Art* 496). I find myself on that same fence concerning the political trajectory of this book. Yet in spite of my commitment to equivocation, my argument is guided as much by an irrational love for the subject as by an honest effort to offer an addendum to Bishop scholarship. My purpose is to demonstrate how and where Elizabeth Bishop's poems and prose lend themselves to a reciprocal reading of artistic form and social function—an easy enough, if not common, critical task. Yet no single twentieth-century poet makes this project so difficult to sustain for such a wide array of readers. The reason has much to do with the work's inherent resistance to definitive, divisive theories of poetic art—sociological, biographical, as well as formalist. And it is this resistance that has kept Bishop attractive to an odd admixture of *lecteurs*: contemporary poets and critics alike often agree that Bishop was one of the best North American poets to emerge in the twentieth century, although they may be at variance as to why.

Just as her poetry will often give way—usually unexpectedly—to prose, her prose comes riddled with "inexplicable" and "always delightful" moments that trouble or expand any narrative or description under way with poetry. But questions of form do not simply resolve themselves in beautiful, autonomous texts; rather, they seem to find expression in human stories, out in the world, where the heroic more often than not resides in the humble. Just as we cannot speak of her poetic form without making room for the antipoetic elements in Bishop's writing, neither can we speak of textual phenomena without considering the social or political immediacy of the "out there" both home and abroad. And in all cases it is wise to stick close to Bishop's language so as not to overlook the slippages and mutinies when and where they occur. When we isolate the personal and public elements of the writing to examine categorically her idiolect or her culture's sociolect, the poetry or the prose escapes us. And without the one, we are left with an incomplete sense of the other.

I hope to convince the reader that there is political merit in paying particularly close attention to the poems' linguistic complexities. The textures of Bishop's poems about foreign travel reveal a consciousness that is fundamentally social, in spite of her reputation for Modernist, ahistorical reserve. If I am suggesting an afterlife for Formalist analysis of Bishop's poetry and prose, it is one that will enhance the important work done by cultural critics since the early 1980s. Because Bishop muddied the waters between the personal and the public in her writing, reading her requires a corresponding commitment to both and a similar trust in "the strange divided singleness" of anyone's experience that John Ashbery recognized early on in her poems (*New York Times Book Review* 8). Her one-eyed, mulatto brother is not an isolated example but rather an embodiment of the idiosyncratic social aesthetic that permeates not only those poems and prose pieces set in foreign places but her work in general.

Part I responds directly to more recent political analyses of Bishop's poetry.[2] I suggest that an early and profound distaste for orthodoxy, especially ideological conformity, had much to do with the aesthetic demands she put on her political convictions. She doubted the motives or capacity for empathy of those who professed their social engagement through altruistic expression or propaganda. Her foreign travels not only continued to reinforce this early skepticism but were instrumental in forming her personal aesthetic as well as her social consciousness. I then encourage more thorough integration of stylistic and linguistic analyses into the reading of Bishop's social consciousness, particularly the political engagement evident in selected poems and prose about foreign travel. If language mattered so much to her, then it may also matter to those who claim to admire her work.

Part II contains three chapters, each of which offers a close reading of a single long poem. Although this limited focus may strike some readers as unnecessarily restrictive, it satisfies a personal, perhaps indulgent taste for reading poems from beginning to end—not something done well in haste. This means not merely snacking on words and phrases but sitting down for a proper, drawn-out, most un-American repast of language. I can only hope my study will make up in depth what it lacks in scope. Travel is the explicit theme that binds these particular poems; political consciousness, internationalist ethics, and human awareness are the implicit themes that tie them together.

Questions of travel bring up questions of form, and because Bishop knows much about both yet is particularly well versed in the latter, she pushes herself in that direction so that, from the vantage gained, she can say something about the ethical and political problems of modern travel. When she asserts herself, and then deftly and only lightly, it is from a vantage gained by an artistry that is scrupulous and hard-won. Our willingness to examine the texture of Bishop's work as well as the plotlines, to look at some of her "apolitical" poems through a political lens, to encounter her prose-poetic style as politically engaged, and finally to look at cases and individuals, not types, can enhance our appreciation of the aesthetic and political challenge Bishop's work continues to offer.

PART I

"The Chameleon's Shameless Interest in Everything but Itself"

Good Liberals, as E. M. Forster knew,
must be liberal enough to be suspicious of being liberal.

—TERRY EAGLETON

Elizabeth Bishop's Social Aesthetic

Distance: Remember all that land
beneath the plane:
that coastline
of dim beaches deep in sand
stretching indistinguishably
all the way,
all the way to where my reasons end?

—BISHOP, "ARGUMENT"

I

IN 1937 HORACE GREGORY PLACED BISHOP'S SHORT STORY "The Sea & Its Shore" as the introductory piece in a volume of *New Masses*. Writing of the selections, Gregory discusses a collaborative approach to Popular Front poetics, a marriage of the writer's abstract imagination with the illuminating, practical skills of the critic.

> Writing of the kind I have selected in this introduction to *New Letters in America* can make few claims to being useful in the day-to-day routine of political discrimination. In that sense any work of the imagination, as distinct from another kind of truth, must always be retranslated into political terms by the political critic, orator, or statesman. There are few occasions when the writer can apply his entire awareness of the world before his eyes to the specific need of immediately political action. (14)

Political potential may lie dormant in a text, not immediately apparent to the reader or the writer until realized or actualized by the literary critic.

Gregory encourages the reader to consider Boomer, the hermit in Bishop's story, the raw material of social commentary as he gathers scraps of fleeting text in the darkness.

> Of course, according to the laws of nature, a beach should be able to keep itself clean, as cats do. We have all observed:
>
> *The moving waters at their priest-like task*
> *Of pure ablution round earth's human shore.*
>
> But the tempo of modern life is too rapid. Our presses turn out too much paper covered with print, which somehow makes its way to our seas and their shores, for nature to take care of herself.
> So Mr. Boomer, Edwin Boomer, might almost have been said to have joined the "priesthood." (*The Collected Prose* 172)

Edwin the hermit, in all the off-center trappings of an allegorical figure, wanders the shore a loaded signifier. A drunken *functioner*, he is also the gatekeeper of lost meaning in an era of excess—perhaps a critic. But without critical interpretation we are at risk, according to Gregory, because such beautiful abstractions are often estranged from the referential, and thus functional, except in those rare cases when writers summon the muse and the musket simultaneously and with equal prowess. In this case the political agenda in "The Sea & Its Shore" needs brokering in the real world, and political critics have been quick to respond to Gregory's invitation to "retranslate" Bishop's work into terms directly useful to current literary theory.

John Palettella, in his article "'That Sense of Constant Re-adjustment': The Great Depression and the Provisional Politics of Elizabeth Bishop's *North and South*," argues that Bishop's politics were grounded in the same skepticism that prevented her from adopting the "cocksure, dogmatic ideology" of masculine heroics in her poems (20, 30). Following James Longenbach's lead, Palettella suggests that Bishop (like Hart Crane and other self-consciously "postmodern" poets of her generation) read T. S. Eliot's poetry and theory of tradition and individual talent very differently from the leading critics of the period:[1] "Whereas New Critics Cleanth Brooks and Robert Penn Warren reread Eliot in 1938 to institute their formalist caveat that 'an organic system of relationships' unifies a poem, Bishop revised Eliot to suggest that texts cohere but never hermetically unify into a still point because of language's provisionality and historical contingency" (24). Palettella turns to this passage from "Dimension for a Novel," which Bishop published in the *Vassar Journal of Undergraduate Studies* in May 1934, as evidence of her very postmodern approach to Eliot and of the fluid, nonlinear "progression" of language and history: "We live in great whispering galleries, constantly vibrating and humming, or we walk through salons with mirrors where the reflections between the narrow walls are limitless, and each present moment reaches immediately and directly the past moments, changing them both" (98–99). Perspective adapts to conditions that are themselves adapting. Thus, because political history is constantly adjusting to the language we use to inscribe it just as language is adapting to the historical peculiarities of the moment, equally flexible modes of reading may be required to locate the political in the rhetorical.

Bishop's undergraduate reading of Eliot helped her understand this.[2] Historical topicality in poetry, in this case, becomes less impressive as a referential sign of political engagement—suspect even, if one distrusts appearances. Social consciousness manifests itself in various guises and attitudes vis-à-vis the downtrodden. In early prose pieces such as "Chimney Sweepers" and "Then Came the Poor," Palettella argues, Bishop took on oppressive social institutions by advocating a personal kind of social justice through a style of writing that "conjoins perspectives without dissolving each perspective's specificity—a form that resists the political certainty and dogma of the otiose 'Word'" (26).

Bishop's direct experience of economic hardship in her early years in Nova Scotia and then during her travels there as a student helps prevent her theory of experiential provisionality from resembling what would later become the tautological rhetoric of academic deconstruction—the playful punning that in the eyes of some New Historicists would align deconstruction with the apolitical discourse of Formalism. In a 1966 interview with her friend Ashley Brown, Bishop remembers the difficult social conditions of the 1930s, conditions she felt many of her professed Marxist classmates had never experienced in any form but the abstract:

> I was aware of the Depression—some of my family were much affected
> by it. After all anybody who went to New York and rode the Elevated
> could see that things were wrong. But I had lived with poor people and
> knew something of poverty at firsthand. About this time I took a
> walking trip in Newfoundland and I saw much worse poverty there.
> (Schwartz and Estess 293–294)

When pushed to locate herself in the "radical political experience of the thirties," however, she continues with characteristic flippancy: "I was all for being a socialist until I heard Norman Thomas speak; but he was so dull. Then I tried anarchism, briefly. I'm much more interested in social problems and politics now than I was in the '30s" (Schwartz and Estess 294). Sidestepping gingerly to avoid ideological confinement, Bishop irreverently mocks the nomenclature of activism by reducing politics to a problem of form.

Although current critics are right to complicate her social convictions to defend her and her aesthetic from simplistic accusations of apolitical elitism, she did not bother to do so herself. In fact, in her later years she seemed to endure interviews only by taunting her audience with bald evasions, as in this interview with Elizabeth Spires in 1978:

> INTERVIEWER: I've been reading a critical book about you that Anne Stevenson wrote. She said that in your poems nature was neutral.
> BISHOP: Yes, I remember the word "neutral." I wasn't quite sure what she meant by that.
> INTERVIEWER: I thought she might have meant that if nature is neutral there isn't any guiding spirit or force.
> BISHOP: Somebody famous—I can't think who it was—somebody extremely famous was asked if he had one question to ask the Sphinx and get an answer, what would it be? And he said, "Is nature for us or against us?" Well, I've never thought about it one way or the other. I like the country, the seashore especially, and if I could drive, I'd probably be living in the country. Unfortunately, I've never learned to drive. I bought two cars. At least. I had an MG I adored for some years in Brazil. (Monteiro 119)

And off she goes to the mountain peaks of Petrópolis and driving lessons. Ill humor or alcohol or both may be directly responsible for this evasive, although concrete, answer to an abstract question, but the impish response is typical of others George Monteiro has compiled in *Conversations with Elizabeth Bishop*. Like Marianne Moore, Bishop frustrated a social scientific appetite for logical connections between theory and art or among history (the MG), philosophy (Nature and Us), and poetry (as usual, reference completely avoided). But like Moore, this reflects less a conscious streak of malice (however present) than a reluctance to reduce enormous questions of human experience to quotations not of her choosing. Spires perhaps appreciated the associative movement of Bishop's mind. Many poems, like oracles, engage history elliptically, and Bishop trusted readers would understand that questions of being, like questions of social consciousness, are sometimes better explored through the trial and error of fluctuating identities than through the confident objectives of political ideology.

II

Betsy Erkkila agrees with Palettella in his assertion that Bishop cultivated a subject-subject mode of socialism hitherto overlooked by critics. In her article "Elizabeth Bishop, Modernism, and the Left," Erkkila argues that in poems like "Cootchie" and "Faustina" and in prose pieces like "Gregorio Valdes," Bishop "comes closer to negotiating the putative conflict between proletarianism and aesthetics than other more earnest commentators on the respective claims of politics and art" (291). While others were arguing over Whitman and James, "She was looking closely and quietly at factory workers" and their "literal, mimetic working class art," which she found "mysterious, uncanny, and alluring" in spite of its humble origins. If Bishop's reflections toward the conclusion of "Gregorio Valdes" (1939), however, do not patronize or sentimentalize the "primitive" artist, neither do they objectify him by confining his identity within the perimeters of socioeconomic class.

Bishop celebrates Valdes in terms she would use for those she admires, terms that often ground the religious in the ordinary:

> There are some people whom we envy not because they are rich or handsome or successful, although they may be any or all of these, but because everything they are and do seems to be all of a piece, so that even if they wanted to they could not be or do otherwise. A particular feature of their characters may stand out as more praiseworthy in itself than others—that is almost beside the point. Ancient heroes often have to do penance for and expiate crimes they have committed all unwittingly, and in the same way it seems that some people receive certain "gifts" merely by remaining unwittingly in an undemocratic state of grace. It is a supposition that leaves painting like Gregorio's a partial mystery. But surely anything that is impossible for others to achieve by effort, that is dangerous to imitate, and yet, like natural virtue, must be both admired and imitated, always remains mysterious. (*The Collected Prose* 58–59)

The value of Gregorio Valdes's painting lies not simply in its naive or unconscious picturesque quality—a more predictable Eurocentric observation of "primitive" art—but rather lies in its testimony to the illusive and somehow ethical makeup of good art.

Yet Bishop throws a wrench into this very classical theory of the plastic arts—now considered rather dangerous—by applying the language used to describe "masterpieces" to the creations of a poor sign painter. Here Bishop negotiates "the putative conflict between proletarianism and aesthetics" by ignoring the historically and culturally distinct contexts of Classical Tragedy, Christian martyrdom, and "ethnic" working-class art. Locating common ground in Grace—as "undemocratic" as it is democratic in that it is blind to material, or worldly, success—Bishop does not so much mystify Valdes's achievement as she insists, perhaps unwittingly, that we consider the value of his work in whatever terms we deem necessary, even if it means breaking into the exclusive lexicon of the aesthetic.

Bishop's fascination with (and sometimes revulsion toward) things Brazilian Catholic often inspires similar flights of classical eloquence, or at least similar strains of Homeric ingenuity. Mystery exists less to be explained than admired when we come into contact with it, in the window of a barbershop: "The picture leaned against a cardboard advertisement of Eagle Whiskey, among other window decorations of red-and-green crepe-paper rosettes and streamers left over from Christmas and the announcement of an operetta at the Cuban school—all covered with dust and fly spots and littered with termites' wings" (*The Collected Prose* 51).

Erkkila encourages us to read Bishop as a writer who resisted the "exalted notion" of the opposition of the role of art and the artist in the modern world—the crime Modernism had been accused of, particularly concerning practical politics. The scene described is less a critique of the dirty working world that art transcends than a fascinated glance at the "cheerful" and "awful" clutter of a culture that surrounds, gives rise to, and manages to honor painting. It is in such ways that Bishop's brand of social engagement extended the personal into the realm of the public, thereby "render[ing] obsolete" the "artificial distinction" between "a public and private poet" (Ashbery in Erkkila 303).

III

Ulterior to both Palettella's and Erkkila's historicized or politicized readings of Bishop, however, is the conviction that the social consciousness movement of the 1930s had a direct effect on Bishop's developing aesthetic. Also embedded in the theory that generates these writers' "retranslations" are other fundamental assumptions: one, that the political atmosphere of the period had an inevitably positive effect on writers in general; and two, that valuable or socially responsible writing can only emerge from the "right" politics, traces of which can be located in Bishop's hitherto underappreciated political agenda. It could be argued, however, that Bishop's rejection of the "social-conscious" discourse of the 1930s and 1940s may be precisely what allowed her to sharpen her idiosyncratic form of political discourse. Although both Palettella and Erkkila give a wide and fair berth to the "dazzling dialectic" of Bishop's relationship to the Left, extending the idea of Feminist and Queer theorists that Bishop moved beyond binarism in all its various guises, they must ultimately adjust their reading of her to suit the objectives of cultural theory.[3]

If Bishop resisted political rhetoric as she did Feminist and sexually explicit rhetoric, her "aversion" was grounded in the same skepticism that helped prevent her poetry and prose from calcifying into a form of dogmatism that could impede speculation. Erkkila acknowledges Bishop's doubts about Communist Party ideology but connects them directly to her "first-hand experience" of the "desecrations" of 1936 Spain. Citing a minor poem, "Lullaby for the Cat" (1937)—Darling Minnow, drop that frown / Just cooperate, / Not a kitten shall be drowned / In the Marxist State (290)—Erkkila attempts to contextualize Bishop's skepticism in a particular historical event, and in doing so she willfully ignores the potentially deeper roots of Bishop's personal distaste for party politics.

Writing in 1940 from Key West, Bishop complained of the unsavory atmosphere created by ideological debate that, she felt, overlooked the integrity of the individual: "I am utterly disgusted with 'social-conscious' conversation—by people who always seem to be utterly unconscious of their surroundings, other people's personalities, etc. etc. I am going to take him [James Farrell] to church to see if I can instill a little respect" (*One Art* 87).

Taking this final dose of religiosity with a grain of salt ("I dislike the race," she once said of ministers in general), she suggests, however offhandedly, that even the church might offer a more humane solution to problems of social exclusion than the party does when the latter's civic habits become self-indulgent (*One Art* 621). The best-intentioned conceptual philosophy was not worth its weight in pamphlets if politics became an end in itself. Dissociating the human face, the frustratingly illogical face of human suffering, from the beautiful logic of earnest propaganda was to elide the subject to ensure the good of the whole. Although this was a necessary evil for some, a writer like Bishop found herself ill equipped to assume the role of public bard, particularly if it meant disengaging herself from her immediate environment. As a writer trusting in particulars, Bishop had no choice but to suspect and reject generalities of human experience, however noble the intentions, as she carried on her slow, subject-to-subject consideration of loss or defeat.

We see her doubt, even as she admires the gloomy but earnest Marxist, Rachel (alias "Mr. Hearn"), in her short story/memoir "The USA School of Writing":

> "Realism" and only "realism" impressed *her*. But if I tried to imply, in
> my old classroom manner, that there was "realism" and "realism," or ask
> her what she *meant* by "realism," she would glare at me savagely, her
> eyes glittering under Stewart's lighting fixtures, and silently stretch her
> large mouth over the bulging tiers of a sandwich. Her mole moved up
> and down as she chewed. At first I was afraid of those slap-like glares,
> but I grew used to them. And when one day, back in our office, she
> asked me to read one of her sentences to see if the grammar was right, I

knew that she had begun to like me in spite of my bourgeois decadence and an ignorance of reality that took refuge in the childishness of anarchism. I also knew she had already sensed something fishy about my alleged political views. (*The Collected Prose* 39–40)

Like the cagey, although tragic, figure Norine, whom Mary McCarthy casts in *The Group*—her illuminating, if sensationalized, depiction of the post-Vassar period in which Bishop herself figures obliquely—Rachel's view of the human soul is as myopic as her vision of social justice is vast.[4] If Norine is politically astute and personally duplicitous, Rachel is equally unable to bridge public conviction and personal honor; in either case the pragmatic heroism of both is undermined by their uselessness in the practical world of individual personalities interacting intelligently with one another.

The popularity of 1930s social realism may have influenced Bishop's early prose in Vassar College publications; she would always maintain a clear, almost calculated sense of audience—even as a "*New Yorker*" poet.[5] Yet to credit the inception of Bishop's social awareness to the Marxist thirties is to overestimate her relationship to the circulating ideology and corresponding rhetoric of her college years. Because topical references, like clothes, go in and out of fashion, Bishop from an early age trusted in classical lines. And in the case of ethics, her reference was perhaps less Marx than Plato and Aristotle—although one could argue that all three eventually agree on the ends, if not the means, of man's self-determination. Eunice Clark Jessup remembers Bishop and Mary McCarthy studying Greek and Latin while she and their classmates "were agitating about world affairs, reading newspapers, debating socialism," even as McCarthy recalls that conversations with Bishop opened her eyes to the socialist argument (Jessup and McCarthy in Fountain and Brazeau 49, 48).

Her college classmates' lack of consensus over Bishop's political position carries on into her adult life: friends and editors simultaneously describe her as deeply compassionate about social injustice and coolly apolitical. Whereas this interpretative discrepancy works both for and against her, depending on one's agenda, it is indicative of the complexity of her positions and her idiosyncratic approach to socialism. Bishop put pressure on the increasingly misdirected dictates of Stalinist Marxism by insisting that the debate remain human and respectful of the human hunger for intellectual as well as aesthetic complexity. To tailor personality as well as poetry to the requirements of general consumption was to lose sight of the ends of poetry, ends sometimes as distant from the requirements of our actual political systems as they are intrinsically involved in the chaos of everyday living. Yet to reduce the purpose of art to immediate human utility was to underestimate the potential political strengths of the enigmatic.

IV

If we agree that the social-conscious writing of the 1930s had less to do with Bishop's variety of ethical dialectics than has been proposed but that social protest resonates throughout the work, how and where do we "retranslate" her poetry into politics? Bishop's experience of poverty as a child in Nova Scotia with her maternal grandparents, and then her experience of wealth in Massachusetts with her paternal grandparents, gave her early and immediate access to the realities of economic disparity. The fact that her best childhood memories and closest family alliances would always be of and with her poorer Canadian relations may have further reinforced the affinity with the dispossessed that permeates her work. But Bishop's early experience of crossing national borders would also establish and then maintain her social consciousness.

First she traveled between Canada and the United States; later she would move often, although never regularly, between Europe and the United States, the East and West Coasts, and—most important—Brazil and everywhere else. As an adult she maintained four principal homes: the first in Key West (one of the "three loved houses" made famous in her villanelle "One Art"); the second in Samambaia, Brazil; the third in Ouro Prêto, Brazil; the fourth and final in Boston. Yet home was a fluctuating concept—a topic she addresses in her poem "Questions of Travel"—and she traveled ceaselessly, if not compulsively, all her life. Travel in Bishop's poems "is a metaphor for our finding out in what relation to the world we exist," says the poet Mark Strand who visited Bishop in Brazil (Strand in Schwartz 242). But that relation for Bishop would always remain intercultural in scope. Her international focus put increased pressure on her national allegiances—particularly when national movements proved culturally insular, even in the service of progressive politics.

In the late 1950s and the 1960s, for example, Bishop found herself increasingly estranged from the hubbub of politics and art on the West Coast. She writes to Lowell complaining of what she feels to be the reactionary aesthetics of the San Francisco Beat movement: "[I]t's terribly hard to find the exact and right and surprisingly enough, or un-surprisingly enough, point at which to revolt now[.] The Beats have just fallen back on an old corpse-strewn or monument-strewn battle-field—the real protest I suspect is something quite different—(If only I could find it)" (Erkkila 304).

Preferring the company and poetry of Thom Gunn to those of Kenneth Rexroth while living in San Francisco in 1968 and 1969, Bishop had reservations about the aesthetic potential of the oral, revolutionary prose-poetry of Allen Ginsberg, at least for herself. In spite of its subversive, antigovernment stance, which she approved of, the Beat movement was the kind of popular arts movement that could easily be co-opted when necessary (*One Art* 496).

Accessibility has its downside. Back in Ouro Prêto in the spring of 1969, Bishop notes the absence of American support for a popular annual Arts Festival there—an absence that could be remedied, she suggests, if the Brazilians would only keep up with current trends in North American arts culture: "We see that all the embassies of Canada, Czechoslovakia, France, Germany, etc., have all contributed to this Arts Festival—but not the U.S.A. WHY? I wonder. . . . Maybe one should consider it all a 'happening'" (*One Art* 507).

This casual aside could be read as the grumbling of an aging artist who no longer sees herself dancing on the cultural edge, or it can be read as an acute assessment of the weaknesses of a counterculture that repeats the sins of its fathers through a simple process of inversion. By privileging social commentary over aesthetics, artists (or literary critics) run the risk of exclusion, however unintentional. As Bishop knew in the 1930s as well as in the 1960s, isolationism, like socialism, comes in many forms—and North Americans, in spite of their enthusiastic desire to change the world, often have a vague working sense of either.

V

In his essay "The Poet and the City," W. H. Auden writes that "the notion of *l'art engagé* and art as propaganda are extensions" of the "heresy" that "utility without gratuity was sufficient to produce art" (*Dyer's Hand* 76). This was a dishonest notion, he claims, grounded in the vanity of writers and their nostalgia for a past "when poets had a public status." Although we must be wary of anything the chimerical Auden says on the topic of socialism, we note a categorical prejudice against social-conscious writing as it was prescribed in the 1930s, a prejudice Bishop shared. The primary problem with political poetry, says Auden, is that it is written by poets; and poets are, "by the nature of their interests and the nature of artistic fabrication, singularly ill-equipped to understand politics or economics" (84). He continues with this materialist, although humorously sweeping, even blasphemous, description of the less glamorous, less heroic side of writing poetry in a modern culture:

> Their [poets'] natural interest is in singular individuals and personal
> relations, while politics and economics are concerned with large
> numbers of people, hence with the human average (the poet is bored to
> death by the idea of the Common Man) and with impersonal, to a great
> extent, involuntary, relations. The poet cannot understand the function

of money in modern society because for him there is no relation between subjective value and market value; he may be paid ten pounds for a poem which he believes is very good and took him months to write, and a hundred pounds for a piece of journalism which costs him but a day's work. (84)

And this final economic reality, he jokes, leads to the political reality behind the aesthetics/activism split in the arts—especially if one reads them in capitalist terms:

> If he is a successful poet—though few poets make enough money to be called successful in the way that a novelist or playwright can—he is a member of the Manchester school and believes in absolute *laissez-faire*; if he is unsuccessful and embittered, he is liable to combine aggressive fantasies about the annihilation of the present order with impractical day dreams of Utopia. Society has always to beware of the utopias being planned by artists *manqués* over cafeteria tables late at night. (84)

Auden takes no pains to side with either extremity of the political spectrum, the laissez-faire elite or the utopists. Shelley's dream of the Poet-Legislator, a dream Auden recognizes in the demands of Leftist critics, however, is put under playful scrutiny.

Like Bishop, Auden doubted the public role of the poet because the immediate needs or expectations of public policy put pressure on poetic production that both knew could have devastating effects on the material— "A poem which was really like a political democracy . . . would be formless, windy, banal and utterly boring" (*Dyer's Hand* 85). Like Bishop, Auden both loved and loathed Whitman. Yet conversely, a body politic structured like a Formalist poem would be equally flawed and even more dangerous:

> A society which was really like a good poem, embodying the aesthetic virtues of beauty, order, economy and subordination of detail to the whole, would be a nightmare of horror for, given the historical reality of actual man, such a society could only come into being through selective breeding, extermination of the physically and mentally unfit, absolute obedience to its Director, and a large slave class kept out of sight in cellars. (*Dyer's Hand* 85)

If Auden parodies the essentialist urge to equate form and content—a tendency indulged in by New Critics and poststructuralist critics alike— then, like Bishop, his argument with social-conscious writing is not so much one of content but of form. Social consciousness in poetry could be accessible in mimetic terms, but often it came folded in the semiotic complexities of individual poems—and these were the poems that mattered most because they placed demands on readers' minds and hearts that referential language could not. Reading, not poetry, was the primary literary problem in postindustrial America.

Wallace Stevens, who like Bishop did not go through a self-proclaimed "revolutionary" period as Auden did and whose poetry therefore—like Bishop's—has had to speak largely for itself while awaiting retranslation, came under heavy fire from the intellectual Left from the earliest reviews of *Harmonium*. Agitated by what was perceived to be Stevens's apolitical aesthetic, many reviewers and critics—both in the 1920s and in the 1980s and 1990s—dismissed him as a dandy and a mouthpiece of the conservative establishment.[6] Directly addressing his critics in "The Noble Rider and the Sound of Words," Stevens had this to say about the intellectual state of working-class America:

> The way we work is a good deal more difficult for the imagination than the highly civilized revolution that is occurring in respect to work indicates. . . . As for the workers, it is enough to say that the word had grown to be literary. They have become, at their work, in the face of machines, something approximating an abstraction, an energy. . . . The time must be coming when, as they leave the factories, they will be passed through an air-chamber or a bar to revive them for riot or reading. (*The Necessary Angel* 19)

Rather than shirk social responsibility, Stevens, like Bishop, believed the poet contributed to the general good by insisting—even in the face of justifiable criticism from the Left—that if physical suffering threatened to reduce people to automatons or children, there was still something in every human being and every reader—however unfortunate—that would impose its subjectivity in spite of external conditions. Suffering had a personality, however depleted, and identifying the individual with her material conditions was necessary in order to organize, but it could not account for or address all the complexities of human survival.

If the word had become too literary, and certainly it had, the writer could respond only by putting pressure on the reader, not by reducing pressure on the language. The latter was precisely what was already happening: As experience was leveled out to suit the purposes of industry, language—like the imagination—was threatening to become more and more stifled. Stevens considers this in abstract terms in such poems as "The Idea of Order at Key West," in which the singer and the song rely on each other for their very existence; or "Disillusionment of Ten O'Clock," where "people are not going / To dream of baboons and periwinkles" because "None of them are strange" or dream in color in a colorless culture that hinders personality and the individual imagination (*The Collected Poems*).

In her poem "Manuelzinho," published in *Questions of Travel* in 1965, Bishop approaches the problem of power relations between workers and employers from a perspective that troubled her contemporaries and still troubles critics who tend to avoid the poem in their discussions of her social consciousness. Here, like Stevens, she identifies aesthetics with protest.

> Half squatter, half tenant (no rent)—
> a sort of inheritance; white,
> in your thirties now, and supposed
> to supply me with vegetables,
> but you don't; or you won't, or you can't
> get the idea through your brain—
> the world's worst gardener since Cain.
> Tilted above me, your gardens
> ravish my eyes. You edge
> the beds of silver cabbages
> with red carnations, and lettuces
> mixed with alyssum. And then
> umbrella ants arrive,
> or it rains for a solid week
> and the whole thing's ruined again
> and I buy you more pounds of seeds,
> imported, guaranteed,
> and eventually you bring me
> a mystic three-legged carrot,
> or a pumpkin "bigger than the baby." (*The Collected Poems* 96)

The poem has been criticized for its "whiff of noblesse oblige" by those whose own good fortune has perhaps made it difficult for them to laugh about the excruciating power relations that go on between classes in other countries (Bidart in Fountain and Brazeau 141). Or better, by those who are understandably uncomfortable with what may be too easily interpreted as a lighthearted treatment of poverty.

The speaker is "a friend of the writer," Bishop's companion Lota de Macedo Soares, a landed but cash-poor Brazilian aristocrat and social activist; Manuelzinho is the actual gardener who lived on the grounds of the Samambaia house in the hills above Rio de Janeiro during Bishop's fifteen-year residence in Brazil. Bishop underscores several points about the landowner's attitude toward her tenant-squatter, the first being that whatever the official terms of the relationship, the actual realization of them has taken its own course, and the landowner is at once exasperated and delighted by this fact. If the speaker begins by delineating the hierarchical structure of the estate, she also hurries to dissemble it by directing our attention to a subject that threatens order or renders it obsolete for the moment: aesthetics—the stunning, illogical mélange of silver cabbage and red carnations "ravishes" the speaker's eyes, and we understand that her inability to direct Manuelzinho's production leads less to chagrin than to a sense of joy.

It is in the tenant's character, however, that we note the poem's respect for its subject. Although we grasp Manuelzinho's personality in terms of his environment, what he will and will not respond to cannot be reduced to categories of the social sciences. Like Cain, he has a legitimate grievance with the powers that control the garden, but he will not be displaced, although his horticultural experiments reflect his fugitive status. His personality impresses on his external conditions and brings forth "mystic" vegetables. Bishop does not romanticize or patronize the gardener. In the final stanza, the speaker confronts her own uneasy authority and questions the platitudinous language she uses too easily to inscribe "her" squatter and their relationship:

> You helpless, foolish man,
> I love you all I can,
> I think. Or do I?
> I take off my hat, unpainted
> and figurative, to you.
> Again I promise to try. (*The Collected Poems* 99)

The question of responsibility lies at the heart of this "elitist" poem, and in this case the promises being made are understood as socially responsible only if Manuelzinho matters to us as much as he does to the speaker at the end of the poem. How we interpret the elitism of the poem will depend on whether we choose to register the socioeconomic inequities of the speaker-subject relationship or the wry heroics and steady will of the subject. The writer directs us to do both. Thus what may appear to be a light narrative poem that perceives the title character "too comfortably as helpless and funny" is actually a complex consideration of class that in this case shuns the more serious garb of social-conscious writing (Bidart in Fountain and Brazeau 141). Manuelzinho paints his straw hat gold and then green; Bishop appreciates the protest and records the individual subject's subversion of authority through aesthetics.

VI

In the conclusion of *The Ideology of the Aesthetic*, Terry Eagleton's study of the intellectual history of Western aesthetics, he argues that in spite of the rejection in poststructuralist thought of "the aesthetic" and all other *grands recits* of the Enlightenment, theories of the beautiful and the sublime can still offer a model for a materialist ethics. "If we do not live in such a way that the free self-realization of each is achieved in and through the free self-realization of all," he argues, then not only will we never realize the objectives of Marx, but we will most likely destroy ourselves as a species (412). This highly abstract counsel can be best observed not by sweeping ideology, he says, but by "actual historical context" or "concrete ethical life, Hegel's *Sittlichkeit*," which means "negotiating and renegotiating, from one specific situation to another," just what free self-realization can mean (412).

Although shying away from broader ideological discussions of subjectivity, Bishop nevertheless remains deeply concerned with the self-realization of individuals in her poems, particularly when that self-realization unfolds in the interstices of culture and class. In "Manuelzinho" we may not receive a clear message about the evils of modern feudalism, and the proof is that few can agree on where the speaker crosses the line into indifference. This uncertainty over "authorial intention" is precisely what the poem addresses. Although the speaker vacillates between contempt and awe, she also recognizes that she can pull rank only in the context of her own discourse. Fighting the speaker all the way, Manuelzinho impresses his "self" on the poem with the obstinate passion of a mute painter. Eagleton underscores the materialist ethics of such a human depiction of struggle:

> The aesthetic is preoccupied among other things with the relation between particular and universal; and this is also a matter of great importance to the ethico-political. A materialist ethics is "aesthetic" in that it begins with concrete particularity, taking its starting-point from the actual needs and desires of individual human beings. But need and desire are what render individuals non-identical with themselves, the medium in which they are opened out to a world of others and objects. The particular from which one begins is not a self-identity—a point which traditional aesthetics, in its eagerness to banish desire from sensuous concretion, is unable to appreciate. This particular individual is self-transgressive; desire springs to birth through our material implication with others, and so will finally give rise to questions of reason and justice, of which and whose desires should be realized and which constrained. It also gives rise to the question of education and transformation of what desires we have, which lies at the centre of a radical politics. (413–414)

Bishop's "negotiating and renegotiating, from one specific situation to another" in "Manuelzinho" and other poems set in foreign places can perhaps be traced to a materialist ethics that owes more to her individual aesthetic and her relationship with foreign people and places than to any clear allegiances she may have felt to the social consciousness movements of the 1930s or the 1960s. Her subjects or particulars are implicitly concerned with self-transgression as they negotiate, even clash, with the material implications of their existence. Desires assert themselves, demand recognition. Yet her scope remains as modest as her professed politics.

Contemporary critics may find they must "retranslate" Bishop to make her suitable for a politically progressive audience, even if Bishop herself firmly rejected the terms in which they conduct the apology. Reading, of course, is always a form of retranslation. But because transgression comes in many colors, as Manuelzinho shows us, we should trust Bishop more than we do to define her radical politics in her own terms. As a writer, Bishop believed in the ethical dialectics of the aesthetic. The literal particulars she offers in her poems do not deflect the personal and the political, as many have claimed, but rather ground both in a temporary, shared reality always implicated in the ethical. Yet if her ethics are never as clearly depicted as her foreign landscapes, it is because she trusts in studied selflessness, or, in the words of her friend Randall Jarrell, in "the chameleon's shameless interest in everything but itself," to explore the connections between things and ideas, the personal and the political (*Poetry and the Age* 142).

2

The Ethics of Travel

630 Dey Street
Key West, Florida
January 1, 1948

I seem to be talking to you like Dorothy Dix but that is because you apparently are able to do the right thing for yourself and your work and don't seem to be tempted by the distractions of traveling—that rarely offers much at all in respect to work. I guess I have liked to travel as much as I have because I have always felt isolated and have known so few of my "contemporaries" and nothing of "intellectual" life in New York or anywhere. Actually it may be all to the good.

—BISHOP TO ROBERT LOWELL, ONE ART 154

I

BISHOP WAS NOT A TRAVEL WRITER PER SE. While she assumed her travels would feed her writing and hoped to continue to partially support herself through her writing, she did not go abroad with the express intention of recording her experiences as many of her contemporaries did, particularly after World War II. In fact, after she had settled in Brazil she feared her South American subjects would eventually work against her: she predicted she would find herself marginalized by the New York literary establishment as a chronicler of the exotic and "picturesque" rather than as a writer who trusted in direct experience for subject matter, wherever found. And neither did she wish to become a poet who could "only write about South America" (One Art 384). "It is one of my greatest worries now," she writes to Robert Lowell in 1960, "how to use everything and keep on living here, most of the time, probably—and yet be a New Englander herring-choker bluenoser at the same time" (One Art 384). Yet it is precisely this unpremeditated or reluctant positioning vis-à-vis her foreign subject that makes Bishop such a fine travel writer. Just as Bishop avoided categorical political

25

positioning in her college years, so would she question the agendas of North Americans who went abroad with vague or whetted dreams of cultural colonialism. In fact, this line of questioning, this weighing of the consequences of relegating unfamiliar landscapes to familiar tropes, constitutes the ethical center of her oeuvre in general and her poems and prose written about foreign places and people in particular.

The popularity of travel writing as a genre has waxed and waned in the West, and it is no surprise to many that travel narratives have become particularly marketable in North America at the turn of the twenty-first century. Many compare this rise to that of the expatriate literature at the turn of the nineteenth century and again to that of post–World War II America when many writers went abroad. In all three cases, it could be argued, the rise of travel writing has come hand in hand with the mobility that power affords. But this recent surge in travel writing is accompanied by an equal and opposing flow in Euro-American cultural theory that labors to historicize and politicize the genre in ways that make it impossible for conscientious readers to assume the neutrality of texts by or about Americans abroad.

Travel writing is an important subject of colonial and postcolonial studies, and any consideration of Bishop's inadvertent contribution to the field must take into account some of the critical tropes that have become the organizing principles by which travel texts—literary and other—are assessed.[1] And although few travel texts—old or new—appear to emerge unbruised or unabashed by such critical scrutiny, Bishop's poems and prose continue to hold up relatively well. In our desire to resist the cultural ravages of multinational corporatism, we listen for those voices that speak of the complexities of self-determination, particularly when the voices appear to avoid the subject in obvious, thus exploitable, ways. In her own questions of travel, Bishop anticipates political, social, and economic theories of travel that would germinate but not come to fruition under the formal rubric of postcolonial studies until after her death in the late 1970s. Bishop understood the hazards of foreign travel; she knew firsthand about the dangers of privileged observation. The risk was not to the observer, as many adventure writers would have us believe. Rather, the real risk was always to the observed.

Although the problems of Euro-American travel writing can be approached in many ways, contemporary cultural theory concentrates on the Eurocentric and imperialistic unconscious—some less "conscious" than others—of the genre. Traditional white male travel texts have tended to treat the foreign or exotic landscape as a museum piece, "as setting," Elizabeth Bohls suggests, "for disinterested aesthetic contemplation, deliberately sequestered from ordinary life" (*Women Travel Writers* 10). This Romantic approach to travel writing has historically elided the relation of aesthetics to the "material, social, and political conditions of human existence" (*Women Travel Writers* 10). And in doing so, travel writing has served to reinforce colonial control by functioning as an instrument within colonial expansion. The tradition of travel writing, and the reading of it, have always been entangled with the creation and maintenance of imperialism, European and other.

This entanglement is not accidental. According to both Michel Foucault and Edward Said, those who wield power in the world prescribe the conventions by which the less powerful are known, at least by the conqueror. Such a reordering of the world's particulars emerges as a constructed knowledge grounded not upon divine intervention or moral superiority or the absence of either but rather upon political or economic circumstance. Thus to travel and record within the imbalances of worldly power can never be a purely aesthetic affair.

Bishop differs from many of her contemporaries and predecessors in the field of travel literature because she approached the subject fully conscious of her position as a colonial writer. To be a "First World" North American after World War II and to write from within about circumstances without was to write against the discourse of political victory and expansion. Talented writers like Bishop—and friends who also lived abroad in the 1950s and 1960s, such as Robert Lowell and James Merrill—were weighted with the responsibility of testing the necessary arrogance of new power against the real, thus inscrutable, knowledge of the outside world. "What travel books are about," says Paul Fussell, "is the interplay between observer and observed, between a traveler's own philosophical biases and prejudices and the tests those ideas and prejudices endure as a result of the journey" (126). Bishop's work has an objectivity that has led some readers, depending on periods in critical or arts fashion, to describe her writing as cold or ahistorical. Yet this same lack of subjective disclosure or topical reference has always struck many, particularly other writers, as one of the most attractive qualities of the writing. Because Bishop labored to expose the philosophical biases of the Western traveler in her poems and prose, it was necessary to cultivate a certain selflessness that could be mistaken for cold critical distance. Yet this ability to decenter the self, even at the risk of disappearing into the nominal detail, gives Bishop's travel literature its focus. It is not necessarily "the interplay between observer and observed" that we witness in her work—a common preoccupation of travel literature, or at least its primary source of interest for the reader; rather, we note a highly conscious consideration of the processes of observation, processes implicated in the dangers of the ahistorical universalization of others.

As the United States began to displace in earnest Europe's claim to cultural hegemony after World War II, American poets began to travel. "If

Europe was dying," suggests Robert Von Hallberg in "Tourism and Postwar Poetry," "so were the former keepers of imaginative vision" (141). Thus American artists, "self-conscious tourists, with a mission," had to take over the responsibility of tending the world's monuments (141). He notes, however, that Bishop and Lowell, even though they ultimately served the purposes of national culture, were two of the few American poets in the 1950s writing with a sense of "imperial doom" (145).

This "doom" Von Hallberg registers can also be described as a social critique of American expansionism. Whereas other writers wrote enthusiastically of the growth of American industry and cultural influence in the aftermath of the Great War, Bishop remained conspicuously silent on the subject of the U.S. victory. When she does approach the Northern continent in any direct form, the critical stance is subtle, rarely—if ever—topical. Yet in spite of her famous reticence, Bishop's travel writing anticipates concerns eventually taken up by postcolonial theorists. The poems I will discuss in detail in Part II of this book specifically address the connection between aesthetic practices and the material conditions of human existence. They explore the ways in which political and economic power relations create one nation's knowledge of another. And the poems and prose anticipate the question Caren Kaplan poses in her book *Questions of Travel* (after Bishop's poem), namely, "how is it possible to avoid ahistorical universalization and the mystification of social relations that Euro-American discourses of displacement often deploy"? (3). Or, in other words, what are the ethical consequences of cultural arrogance?

In "Over 2,000 Illustrations and a Complete Concordance," Bishop predicts Fredric Jameson's notion of pastiche as the cannibalism of images (Matos 220). In this long poem, written over a ten-year period and finally published in 1955, Bishop guides us through the processes by which real places and the real people who inhabit them are displaced by text—in this case a large, illustrated coffee-table edition of the world's holy sites. Yet in the poem she also reads material culture—ancient ruins—as another kind of text, one that like the literary text ultimately fails to cannibalize the past. Bishop does not moralize this dissolution even as she politicizes it. Rather, she envisions possibilities in the emptying out of referents where others might see only destruction.

Because her travel narratives never attempt to be entirely objective about the objective world, Bishop strikes a balance between the self-conscious gaze of the observer and the physical individual observed. In her poem "Questions of Travel," the interplay between the speaker (not necessarily the writer, as many assume) and the world is the axis on which the poem turns. If the philosophies of Locke and Descartes split the mind and the body—thus clearing the way for modern travel writing that seeks to be objective about the foreign world, only to end up objectifying it—as Casey Blanton and others argue, Bishop herself is wary of such binarisms (Blanton, *Travel Writing: The Self and the World*). The poem "Questions of Travel" questions the speaker's motives for foreign travel:

> Should we have stayed at home and thought of here?
> Where should we be today?
>
> . . .
>
> "Is it lack of imagination that makes us come
> to imagined places, not just stay at home?" (*The Collected Poems* 93–94)

Yet these questions inevitably lead into and out of careful and politicized observations. The nominal details in the poem function as revealed traces of colonization. And the speaker's awareness of this legacy limits the poem's Romantic indulgences as it does the distancing effect of the descriptive chronicling of the landscape.

Reading the world is like writing, and both are like traveling. In "Journeys into Kansas," William Least Heat-Moon discusses the Hopi Indian "maze of emergence," a glyph that "reminds Hopis of the necessity to move away from the self into other things in order to become fully human" (20). Bishop's poems and prose about foreign subjects reenact this struggle to read and to travel beyond the limitations the self imposes upon experience to grasp it clearly and comfortably. Her speakers emerge as human precisely because they fail to control their experience, and in "Questions of Travel" they leave us with no reductive answers to the problems of personal and cultural identity in a postcolonial historical period.

In "Crusoe in England," the third long "travel" poem I discuss in Part II, Bishop imposes herself on a classic text, Daniel Defoe's *Robinson Crusoe*, this time to strip or loosen that text's grip on the historical realities of colonialism. Again she exposes the biases and prejudices endemic to the traveler who, like a turtle, takes his home with him wherever he goes. The poem records a loss of that bias and of the exotic otherness of a place and people when domesticated or destroyed by imperialist expansion. Here as in all her work, the political concerns of Bishop's travel poems cannot be separated from their foreign landscapes any more than they can be considered separately from the self or selves that speak of a place. And everything, both public and personal, is accessible to a reader only through careful scrutiny of the poem's language.

If Kaplan borrows her title from Bishop for her own excellent book on travel and displacement in the wake of modern imperialist expansion, she nevertheless invokes the poem "Questions of Travel"—and, by association, poems of a similar type, time, and place—to bring to light the limited representation of postcolonial travel therein. "Travel is very much a modern concept," Kaplan argues, "signifying both commercial and leisure movement in an era of expanding western capitalism" (3). And Bishop's poem, although it questions Western manifest destiny, "simply destabiliz[es] the notion of home [wherever that may be]" without addressing the "historical question of accountability" (6, 7). This reading of Bishop's poem is troublesome but not surprising. Kaplan notes that her own desire to focus on questions of representation and production of Euro-American contemporary criticism came at a moment of dissatisfaction with the close reading of literary texts (6). It is perhaps because of this dissatisfaction, or waning interest, that Kaplan opts to base her conclusions of the poem's meaning—as well as her text's introduction—on an established reading of a "modernist" classic rather than engage the poem afresh. Thus she can guardedly assert, but assert nonetheless, that Bishop's subjects "are not universal although they can be glibly assumed to be transcendental figures of displacement in a modern world of fragmentation" (7). Bishop's questions are transparent, echoing, as they must, the master narratives of post–World War II, modernist American literature and culture.

In displacing Bishop's literary text with metanarrative, Kaplan does a service to the field of travel writing theory, or theory of displacement, even as she mismanages the poetry through simplified—thus erroneous—assumptions of its scope and depth. This underestimation of Bishop's art hearkens back to the poet's earliest critics, the New Critics—that is, until Marianne Moore and Robert Lowell championed Bishop persuasively enough to the critical community to allow the poet to come into her professional own. One cannot, perhaps, do both—serve literature and theory simultaneously and evenly. Kaplan's introductory comments offer Bishop's poem as codified text, secondary to the cultural query that has displaced the poem as the focus of critical analysis. Thus Kaplan appears to be somewhat comfortable staking her short but significant analysis of the poem on received opinion: Bishop, the modernist poet, harbors "nostalgic," "mythic" dreams of home in the privileged West ("Should we have stayed at home and thought of here?") rather than figuring a "way of being home" that is politically engaged.

II

But Bishop doesn't help us much. Because the majority of the poems and the prose tend to avoid explicit reference to topical issues even as they shower phenomenological details with attention, our best evidence of Bishop's social and international conscience is found in the particulars of her language. Bishop's trust in inductive reasoning may be useful here. Just as the chameleon displays its "shameless interest" in its surroundings by disappearing into them, so do the ethoses of the poems and prose camouflage themselves within the bodies of the texts. And in Bishop's writing this subsumption of the political within the aesthetic is precisely what has ensured its survival.

This is why paying close attention to the physical landscape of the written text only enhances political readings of Bishop. If Bishop chooses to represent "the dispossessed and outcast as subjects" in the traditional forms of high art and this choice complicates the "surface of the texts," as Betsy Erkkila has asked us to believe on good faith—because she offers no textual analysis of such an affinity—the linguistic and semiotic complications of this relationship are perhaps worth exploring if we wish to retranslate Bishop in terms that will satisfy or seduce other cultural critics (Erkkila 285). If Bishop "celebrat[es] the rootless traveler" rather than situating him historically, as Caren Kaplan suggests, it may be advisable to account rhetorically for such an ahistorical reading (7). Critics like Margaret Dickie, who have an interest in linguistic and semiotic analysis yet show signs of old-school Formalism in their final retranslations of Bishop, may serve as warning signs.[2] Formal analyses need not be confined to outmoded definitions of the aesthetic.

The notion of an antithetical relationship between the political and the aesthetic runs contrary to Bishop's understanding of art and travel. Yet our readings based on a critical paradigm of contextualization more often than not bypass the written text, the only empirical evidence we have of a writer's objectives. Although we no longer speak of authorial intention, we still attend to its specter. Poems or prose that destabilize established, unifying metanarratives are still associated with the writers' lives that produced them. And although we admire and recirculate Foucault's death sentences aimed at authors and their intentions, we nevertheless have much to say about what "author functions" desire, condone, or avoid—particularly in matters of sociopolitics.

Because of these textual bypasses, however—which subsequently make room for our own cultural theory of which the poetic text offers a ghostly example of support or repeal—our analyses often read like observations of nineteenth-century anthropologists who elide or undervalue the language of the "natives" to better serve the aims of occidental theories of the subject. Although it can be argued that a lack of historical topicality in Bishop's poems does not necessarily imply a lack of interest in politics (see Palettella) or that Bishop's poems "register" the " 'revolutionary' effects of the time as crisis of the subject, of knowledge, of signification, and of the possibility of meaning itself"—even if she never wrote the topical poems we associate with 1930s social-conscious writing (see Erkkila 285)—such discussions focus almost wholly on the conceptual subject rather than on the effectual registration of such interest or crisis (Erkkila 286). Very good political readings are supported by few close readings of Bishop's language in spite of the structuralist vocabulary scattered throughout the postmodern prose.

Critics choosing to defend Bishop's politics tend to base their discussions on the four most "topical" poems she published. Like other critics who wish to unveil Bishop's hitherto overlooked "radical humanism," they focus on the four or five poems that make clear reference to political or social issues or that Bishop clearly referred to as having political significance—poems such as "Roosters," with its allusions to World War II and concordant male aggression; "A Miracle for Breakfast," which Bishop called her "Depression" poem; "Love Lies Sleeping" and its industrial imagery; and "Pink Dog," a poem about poverty and the temporary cure or cover-up of Carnival.[3] Although it is good that these poems are receiving overdue attention, one wonders why Bishop's other, less obviously political poems are considered less often for what they reveal about her social consciousness. Because writers do not turn their political or social allegiances on and off like a ball and spigot, ideology inhabits—or must precede, as cultural materialists argue—a writer's aesthetic no matter how close to the surface it may appear in a particular poem. To base trust on referential surfaces, therefore, is hardly in keeping with a poststructuralist commitment to the complex function of discourse. One reason for this pattern in Bishop criticism may be that her "renaissance" is still rather new, as Thomas Travisano tells us in "The Elizabeth Bishop Phenomena." He suggests that it is only with Bishop's "coming out" that the "reading public has an image" of a poet "capable of sustaining the impression of a major writer" (920).[4] But this does not address larger questions about the diminished role of the literary in literary criticism.

By letting the text speak, however, trusting that the social or the political will be folded within the language of the poems, we not only support our claims—thus minimizing the generalizations and ungrounded assumptions that weaken theory; we also enhance our own interpretations by constantly testing the acumen of our assertions. By supplementing progressive politics with linguistic analysis, we respect the integrity of Bishop's texts. Vernon Shetley suggests that the poetry of Bishop, Ashbery, and Merrill offers both the public and academics a direction for poetry in an age increasingly indifferent to it.

> [P]oetry can still propose to do what lyric has always proposed to do: to embody subjectivity in shared, public forms; to record the form and pressure of the time upon consciousness, but given that our era is one

dominated, intellectually, by various radical skepticisms, that recording must itself show the mark of those skepticisms, must itself demonstrate the poet's awareness of the corrosive doubt about the nature of
subjectivity itself that thinking people now inhabit. (*After the Death of
Poetry* 29)

As a "skeptical lyricist," Bishop not only puts contemporary pressure on old
suppositions about subjective experience, she also puts poetic pressure on
unsatisfying assumptions about the clear and direct relation between historical content and political forms.

III

Bishop's confounding of divisions of labor in her professional life—she was
never the charismatic teacher Lowell was, although she was equally unsuccessful with her colleagues—is not motivated by any pretensions to change
or undermine the system, as it were.[5] Rather, her unorthodoxies stem from
an unself-conscious aversion to compartmentalize experience, both in her
life and in her work. Her conservative outward appearance said little, or
perhaps everything, about her idiosyncratic brand of revolution, just as the
matter-of-fact physical reality of things may or may not function enigmati-
cally in her poems. In the opening stanzas of "Arrival at Santos," the first
poem in *The Collected Poems*, the prosaic quality of the language contains a
teasing, lyrical undercurrent that surfaces in waves of self-mockery in the
poem:

> Here is a coast; here is a harbor;
> here, after a meager diet of horizon, is some scenery:
> impractically shaped and—who knows?—self-pitying mountains,
> sad and harsh beneath their frivolous greenery,
>
> with a little church on top of one. And warehouses,
> some of them painted a feeble pink, or blue,
> and some tall, uncertain palms. Oh, tourist,
> is this how this country is going to answer you
>
> and your immodest demands for a different world,
> and a better life, and complete comprehension
> of both at last, and immediately,
> after eighteen days of suspension? (89)

This new landscape appears contingent on the eyes of the beholder who sees
in spurts of tentative metaphoric effort, "who knows?—self-pitying mountains," in spite of the general malaise that plagues her as an overambitious

"tourist." Prescribed expectations of the exotic, or, as I will argue, the revolutionary, not only hinder the appreciation of the moment; they put "immodest demands" on reality that say more about the subjective longings of the viewer than the objective experience does.

In this case, however, the existential traveler's blighted expectations are less tragic than funny. The simple two-beat rhythms and syntax of the first line, the anaphoric referent "Here" plus a verb form of "to be," then the subject, "Here is a coast; here is a harbor," remind us of the old ditty and its accompanying hand trick, "Here is the church; here is the steeple." Thus the poem begins not only by reducing the speaker's "quest" to a game of identification for North American children but also by mocking the flat recognitions in language we resort to before we have mustered the rhetoric necessary to inscribe and thus create "adult" experience. Travel is only as foreign as we allow it to be. Our terms expose our capacity for negotiating difference, and in the case of the poem's opening, those terms are markedly limited.

This observation has enormous consequences when considered on an intercultural scale. And Bishop's poems translate into other scales, even if she does not announce such an ambitious project directly. Her poems that confront the paradoxes travel makes evident reveal much about her personal view of human-man as political-man, particularly his fluctuating capacity for recognition. In these first stanzas the speaker's self-mocking desire to immediately recognize a "different world" and a "better life" in a foreign landscape is characteristic of a culture with a vested interest in surfaces. Whether this is a result of our childlike attention span (one result of industrial progress) or a historical habit of reading personal destiny into an impersonal world, or something else, the trust in a direct relationship between worldly signs and their abstract significance is subtly questioned.

In a poem that introduces an entire section of poems about a foreign country, Brazil, a dream of miraculous personal vision is answered with disappointing scenery. This announces something crucial about recognition: it doesn't happen the way we hope it will. It is when Anglo North Americans like "Miss Breen" leave the safety and disappointment of the ports—those highly unreliable and superficial gateways—and drive "to the interior" that things may begin to signify in interesting or critical ways. These things may or may not suit our dreams of "complete comprehension," and in all cases our private readings cannot control all of our experience. Santos, Santarém, or any place the traveler may project her cultural expectations goes on with or without her. And the recognition of this reality is as essential to learning how to observe and respect the "outside" world as it is destructive to the egocentricities that fuel the dreams of empire.

If Bishop's poetry "render[s] obsolete" the superficial distinctions between the personal and the political, as Ashbery maintains, her poems and
prose concerning foreign cultures and landscapes dramatize this dissolution
in particularly engaging ways. Travel coerces the political unconscious to
the surface. Individuals as well as nations find that ideals held true often fall
sadly short of their better, abstract selves when forced into the action foreign involvement demands of them. Bishop knew this from personal experience. And as apolemical as the surfaces of her travel poems and prose may
appear—fortunately, she never *tells* us what she is up to—it is nevertheless
through aesthetic action that we find Bishop engaged in her own examination of social consciousness, even if that examination remains as informal
as the poems are casual.

IV

Close readings of several "travel poems" occupy Part II of this text. Each has
been chosen from a separate collection, and when placed in chronological
order the poems attest to a mature preoccupation with the philosophical
and political implications of living in foreign places among foreign people.
"Over 2,000 Illustrations and a Complete Concordance," "Questions of
Travel," "Crusoe in England," and "Santarém" have many things in common, not the least of which is the experience of otherness—both within
and without—that circulates in the poems and never plays out in predictable ways. These poems record a vulnerability to cultural alienation yet do
not resolve conflict through nostalgia or romantic myths of self-realization.
Bishop avoids drawing morals. Yet the demands Bishop's poems make on
their subjects are easily overlooked because of the seemingly seamless texture of the language.

The language of the poems will occupy the following pages—language
that dares us to penetrate these proselike poems' casual surfaces. Unlike
other, equally admired although perhaps more often anthologized poems (if
anything, for their brevity but most likely for their exemplary Formalism),
these "travel" poems occupy a consistently ambiguous territory between poetic and prosaic language. It is as if questions of travel necessarily bring up
questions of form. To move beyond one's own borders means accepting that
familiar ways of ordering experience may prove futile, and Bishop relaxes
her allegiances to traditional forms to allow herself the space to explore
these new landscapes.

These poems are history lessons, but they are lessons in which the laws
of identity are "put through the hoops," as Octavio Paz writes in a poem
translated by Bishop ("Objects & Apparitions"). The poem is dedicated to
the conceptual artist Joseph Cornell, whom the two writers and friends

admired. Like his boxed collages of found objects, Bishop's oblique lessons come to us in fragments—fragments that like ruins appear to be "the opposite of history." Reading each poem with the patience a decade of writing merits, we are surprised by what we learn about the way meaning gathers itself from the texture of language; how rhythm, syntactical discrepancies, internal rhymes, the consolidation of imagery, and then the sudden lack of any of these tease us into unexpected recognitions. We are not being told to be more sympathetic tourists or more conscientious citizens; neither are we being told to be more actively involved in international trade policy decisions. Rather, we are being trained to read the signs foreign experience offers. We are being shown what it means to be on the outside looking in. We are being educated, however indirectly, as postcolonials about the world and how to travel in it.

PART II

Readings

To look at the stars always makes me dream, as simply as I dream over the black dots of a map representing towns and villages. Why, I ask myself, should the shining dots of the sky not be as accessible as the black dots on the map of France? If we take the train to get to Tarascon or Rouen, we take death to reach a star. One thing undoubtedly true in this reasoning is this, that while we are *alive* we *cannot* get to a star, any more than when we are dead we can take the train.

—VINCENT VAN GOGH, *LETTERS* (273)

3

"Over 2,000 Illustrations and a Complete Concordance"

READING DESERT DUST

I

BISHOP HAD NO FORTUNE, but as a college graduate visiting Europe and parts of North Africa—the first time in 1935 and the second in 1937—she enjoyed the luxury of mobility her moneyed associations helped her afford. Yet even as Bishop sojourned in Paris, sharing an eight-room apartment at 58 rue de Vaugirard—thanks in part to "THE DOWAGER," the wealthy mother of her companion Louise Crane—she was self-conscious about becoming a character in a Jamesian novel (*One Art* 36). Expatriate Americans she came in contact with and wrote home about struck her as unreal fixtures in imagined landscapes, characters in Romantic reenactments of a Europe that existed more in the collective imagination of moneyed America than in the postindustrial twentieth century. She writes to Marianne Moore in 1935:

> We spent four of five days in Paris—one with an American family who now live in one of Madame Pompadour's hunting lodges outside Versailles. The place is exquisite, rather neglected, with pools, foun-

tains, goats and cows around in the fields, among hundreds of weatherbeaten statues, and apple and pear trees that have been trained to grow on the ground or in spirals, or like candelabra. The Americans are just like people out of the movies, so it wasn't as pleasant as it should have been. (*One Art* 34)

The Romantic beauty of the landscape, an attractive Gothic dilapidation that Ruskin or Turner would have appreciated, becomes even further removed from reality when it functions as the backdrop for a period piece starring wealthy Americans. And there is something "unpleasant" about the controlled squalor now possessed and inhabited by picture-perfect people posing as country squires.

Similarly, self-fashioning American men, casting themselves after Wildean or Proustian constructions of "the gentleman," strike twenty-four-year-old Bishop as not only absurd but rather unsavory: "I am not, never, never, an EXPATRI-ATE. We went to a tea at Comtesse de Chambrun's and I met a few men—so languid, so whimsical, so *cultured*—youthfully middle-aged, and reminding me of nothing so much as flourishing fuzzy gray *mold*" (*One Art* 37).

In this offhanded declaration of independence, Bishop communicates what will prove a commitment to the unexpected in her life and work abroad. Men—or women—who cultivate a parasitic, "moldy" relationship with the iconography of a culture do not sustain her interest. They reek of the manufactured, the prescribed. Her complaint is about a mode of representation that repels her not only by its disingenuity but by its reduction of the possibilities of human personality as well as culture.

She prefers the French maid, not only because she is "really very cute" but because she polishes the floor "by putting a cloth down, running and sliding on it," and snorts and titters convulsively every time Bishop speaks French (37). The human detail that trumps expectation attracts Bishop's selective attention. Visiting Douarnenez, a fishing village on the coast of Brittany, Bishop redefines the "picturesque" as something sharpening the sensibilities with solid presence rather than flooding the imagination with vague, Romantic sensations of pleasure: "just like the water in Salt Lake, you simply can't sink in it, it is so strong" (34). "Aquamarine blue" fishnets, Breton costumes at a parade, a seal that "climbed a ladder carrying a lighted lamp with a red silk shade and bead fringe on his nose" are what specifically fascinate Bishop. Her experience abroad is an ongoing confrontation of the extraordinary nominal detail that excites the imagination precisely because the mind seems to have no preexisting category for it.

The categorical response to the picturesque, the "automatic reaction," occupies Bishop throughout her life in her letters, prose, and poems. Concluding another enthusiastic letter to Moore in 1937, this time from Rome,

Bishop finishes a description of the bronze pinecone in the Vatican with this self-mocking reference to the innocuous, although pompous, literature of tourism:

> We have been sightseeing strenuously and systematically and I should like to describe many infinitely described things to you. . . . But in the words of a fascinating guidebook we have, composed mostly of quotations from 18th- and 19th-century travelers, "My presentiment of the emotions with which I should behold the Roman ruins has proved quite correct." (*One Art* 65)

Aware that any recapitulation of a famous scene runs the risk of rhetorical redundancy, Bishop forgoes her own attempt by exposing the machinations of representation. Just as the American family at Versailles or the expatriates at the tea in Paris are hybrid reconstructions, self-reflexive in that their apparent forms are derived from other texts somewhere out of historical time, the act of writing—also a kind of self-fashioning—can become hopelessly caught up in a monotonous replay of receding narratives. Amused by the bold, artificially elevated declaration of this fact in her guidebook, Bishop, a "deconstructionist" before her time, is perfectly aware of the hazards of inscription—how writing, like tourism or self-imposed exile, runs the risk of resuscitating the dullest cultural clichés at the very moment it is trying to escape them.

Bishop made this awareness a subject in her writing. The superficial insights of the picturesque, the automatic, underweighed reaction to foreign experience, point to the complex problems of representation that travel and writing about it pose. To read the foreign subject well and write about it when one has few illusions about one's capacity to step beyond the limitations of culture puts extraordinary pressure on the work—pressure under which language, more often than not, collapses.

In her short prose piece "The Sea & Its Shore," she offers this "collapse" as the moral—however opaque—to her story. Responding to reservations Moore and her mother had about linguistically banal moments in the story, Bishop defends her language by pointing out the ironic intentions behind her choices.

> I have taken over, or gobbled up like a Pelican, everything you suggested except one: "It is an extremely picturesque scene." . . . You say you feel it to be too "automatic." In a way, that was what I meant it to be—I was, I suppose, making fun of an automatic reaction to the scene I was describing and I wanted, as the only "moral" in the story, to contradict, as quietly as possible, the automatic, banal thing that one might have said: "How *picturesque*—He looks like a Rembrandt!" That is, the

conclusion of the sentence, "but in many ways not," is really thought of as being spoken in a different tone of voice. However if this oversubtlety (and, I'm afraid, superiority) on my part did not make itself plain to you, there must be something very wrong and I'm going to try to change it and convey the idea a little more clearly. (*One Art* 54)

The failure and contradiction of "the automatic, banal thing" are the projected "moral." Her protagonist, Edwin Boomer—eccentric, hermit, hero—must be defended against any dull interpretations of the passive on-looker. As keeper of the shore and random scraps of text the sea throws back, something of a priest, something of a poet, he merits the sympathetic response of those who appreciate the complexities of his duties. His strange actions require equally extraordinary readers. He is not simply *nature morte* in "an extremely *picturesque* scene," accessible only through reference to other physical cultural data: "He looks like a Rembrandt!" Yet because this "moral" must be quiet, it takes the form of an aside, a sudden splintering of tone and voice, "but in many ways not."

In the final published version of "The Sea & Its Shore," Bishop uses the "moral" twice. In the first instance, she irons out any obvious or "supe-rior" irony in the section by subsuming the moral aside into the odd, un-even texture of the first-person narrative voice: "Every night he walked back and forth for a distance of over a mile, in the dark, with his lantern and his stick, and a potato sack on his back to put the papers in—a pictur-esque sight, in some ways like Rembrandt" (*The Collected Prose* 172). No italics or exclamatory phrases, yet still the fragmented observation, now couched in an aside whose potential as a moral is hedged with the hesitant "in some ways." In the story's odd conclusion, however, she maintains the original form—in spite of the characteristic deference with which she hon-ored Moore, particularly when Bishop was young. The bland, romantic quali-fier "picturesque" and the distancing allusion to Rembrandt ring false and feel out of place, like sneakered tourists in St. James Cathedral. And the aside, which rejects the "automatic reaction," gets the last word; a final, although quiet, revision of the narrator's earlier hesitation. In a text pre-sumably all about text, Mr. Boomer and his "concentration on the life of letters" still require more devotion to description than the intertextual ref-erence can muster. We may not fully understand him or his enterprise, but when we fall back on the automatic phrase to do our interpretive work for us, we get the reading we earn.

II

The undermining of the "automatic reaction" is the tentative moral of Bishop's poem "Over 2,000 Illustrations and a Complete Concordance," which first appeared in *Partisan Review* in 1948. Yet just as Edwin Boomer, the roving subject of "The Sea & Its Shore," is at the mercy of an onlooker whose voice vacillates between "the automatic, banal thing" and a fresh, rather off-center conspiring of descriptive prose, so the speaker in the poem hesitates between similar interpretive allegiances to its subject. The experiences of foreign travel both attract and repel the speaker. And as the figures become increasingly exotic, her ability to read them becomes increasingly limited.

The speaker's struggles to inscribe her own travels are enveloped within the pages of another book that at first does not and then does offer her a way to read what she cannot understand. It is a big, gilded book of engraved images, similar to the kind Bishop mentions twice in "In the Village" (*The Collected Prose* 246, 265). It is not, as David Kalstone calls it, "a beloved childhood book" but rather an "unlovely," "heavy" encyclopedic text that presumes to identify the world's most important foreign sites within its 2,000 illustrations and complete concordance (*Five Temperaments* 27). It sits on the coffee table or decorates a "cozy corner" and teaches the Occidental family everything it knows about the "Third World" and its shrines ("The Village," *The Collected Prose* 246).

The poem opens with a bold exclamation. And the speaker's first words, an anaphoric reference to the past, throw conditional doubt—mock or serious—on an entire way of experiencing the world. We walk in mid-conversation, mid-text:

> Thus should have been our travels:
> serious, engravable.
> The Seven Wonders of the World are tired
> and a touch familiar, but the other scenes,
> innumerable, though equally sad and still,
> are foreign. . . . (*The Collected Poems* 57)

The introductory question is one of the discrepancies between lived, individual experience and that experience as it appears on the page. The solemn text, with its images first engraved in wood, then pressed to ink and page in a series of receding forms, seems as unlike what the speaker actually witnessed as the scenes that follow. Yet the superiority of the engraved image to actual experience is the first thing we are asked to consider and accept. Certainty, however, is always foreboding in a Bishop poem, especially when it appears too much too soon. The pompous "Thus" and initial marching of the trochees in the first line—depending on how much emphasis we give to the self-chastisement in "should"—signal us that something is already amiss. Such seriousness is suspect, yet the irony is as diffuse and uncertain as that in the "picturesque" scene of Edwin Boomer. It may be verbal irony—we assume there is a discrepancy between what the speaker asserts and what she intends to mean; or it may be dramatic irony, assuming there is a conflict in meaning that we can locate, to which the speaker may or may not be privy. We cannot be quite sure yet.

Things "tired and a touch familiar" are hardly "Wonders" in the American lexicon, where new or virgin tends to be synonymous with holy, so we know we are being teased by the content as well as the form. Yet because we locate almost immediately what feels like the ethical epicenter of the poem—the silliness of time-honored, received images; the kind of data that generate and sustain the "automatic reaction"—we know to wait, to suspend judgment. This poem, like many Bishop poems, unfolds slowly and retroactively. We won't know where we've been until we look again in the rear-view mirror.

The poem then leaves the excessively exposed "Seven Wonders" and considers other lifeless "foreign" figures:

> . . . Often the squatting Arab,
> or groups of Arabs, plotting, probably,
> against our Christian Empire,
> while one apart, with outstretched arm and hand
> points to the Tomb, the Pit, the Sepulcher.
> The branches of the date-palms look like files.
> The cobbled courtyard, where the Well is dry,
> is like a diagram, the brickwork conduits
> are vast and obvious, the human figure
> far gone in history or theology,
> gone with its camel or its faithful horse. (57)

Making fun of Christendom's paranoid obsession with the narrative of the plotting Arab, Bishop reduces the Romantic attitude toward the Islamic world to its fundamental source. The fear and attraction that induced nineteenth-century armchair adventurers to devour George Byron's Romantic tales of Orientalist love, treachery, and conquest in long poems like *The Giaour* give way to a standardized Occidental attitude toward peoples of the Islamic world—our studied denial of their humanity. They squat in the dirt in our travel narratives, less people than signposts indicating other, more important exotic signifiers like "the Tomb, the Pit, the Sepulcher"—places that have more real cultural significance for us than the actual people who live within their midst.

Or do they? Oddly, the poem dedicates more space to these emptied human abstractions than to the holy shrines themselves. There is a pathetic quality about this monumental list that comes at the end of a sentence not dedicated to it and whose capitalized first letters seem a mere formality. We are not invited to observe "the Tomb, the Pit, the Sepulcher." We already know them through reproductions. They, too, are "tired and a touch familiar." Like the "Well" and the "brickwork conduits" that used to feed them, the shrines also seem to have no significance or function, being as "dry" as they are "vast and obvious." Yet it is important to note the lack of nostalgia or "Modernist" despair over lost unifying cultural narratives. These are "diagram[s]" whose distance, so far, is less intensified by superior comparatives to the present than reduced by overexposure. And with this sense of collapsed perspective comes a vague lethargy, something "sad and still." We feel these "barbaric" keepers of our holiest shrines simply attract the speaker's rather world-weary attention more. They at least are exotic. The demonization and concomitant "emptying out" of Muslims as signifiers have survived the Christian crusades, and there they still are—"squatting" and "plotting"—and "though equally sad," at least still picturesque enough to excite curiosity.

Bishop's noncommittal nod to the institutionalized racism that actualizes itself in our most innocent texts is brief. It does not work itself up to the level of a unified "message." It is too early in the poem for anything like that. These Arabs—caricatures in a book of many, as distant as the history and theology they inhabit, as marginal as any cowboy on a "faithful horse"— simply disappear into the genderless, subjectless, subject pronouns from which they came; they become "figures," "its." And as the poem pans further away from the human figure, the textual figure takes over:

> Always the silence, the gesture, the specks of birds
> suspended on invisible threads above the Site,
> or the smoke rising solemnly, pulled by threads.
> Granted a page alone or a page made up
> of several scenes arranged in cattycornered rectangles
> or circles set on stippled gray,
> granted a grim lunette,
> caught in the toils of an initial letter,
> when dwelt upon, they all resolve themselves. (*The Collected Poems* 57)

Just as the human complexity of the Arab figures is silenced in our narratives about the Middle East, so the poem moves to silence the dull figurative plodding of the big book. And as the speaker's observations become more abstract, the text becomes more real in material terms. Emptying out the narrative potential of the images leads to an increased interest in the aesthetic arrangement of the pictures on the page. And then, finally, the entire arranged world of the "Complete Concordance" disappears into the "grim lunette," itself "caught in the toils of an initial letter" or the ornamental, mock-Arabic script so popular in Victorian texts.

In this wonderful new material context we are given the key to the preceding text's perspective. Our travels are already engraved in and by the Occidental narratives that have preceded us into the Holy Land—from those of the eleventh-century crusaders to those of the nineteenth-century Romantics and colonialists. And although the lens we owe our vision to may appear to decorate itself in the more exotic wrappings of the "target" culture, the look is still "grim" and "set on stippled gray." What we have seen has depended on what arrangement on the page the images were "granted." The passive verb appears twice in close proximity—"Granted a page alone or a page made up," "granted a grim lunette." We are thus, in turn, allowed, permitted, *authorized* a certain arrangement of materials, a certain prescribed experience. And we are "granted" this by a subject who is absent because he or she is both everywhere and nowhere, a metanarrative that—godlike—circulates unseen in the collective consciousness even as it manipulates the strings or "threads." Our experiences of travel as text, like the arranged images, the labyrinthine "initial letter," ultimately "resolve themselves" or refer back to themselves rather than to any experience "out there."

As poststructuralists we may be tempted to stop here, concluding that in the poem, travel—like writing—is a self-reflexive game that smacks of cultural hegemony. But this conclusion would serve more the purposes of our own enlightened narratives than the poem. Bishop complicates such a reading with a simple clause. The arranged images only "resolve themselves" "*when dwelt upon.*" Bishop thus affords the speaker the imaginative potential to trace the circuitous script and the intellectual capacity to comprehend when and how culturally manufactured narratives are working on her. Moving from the book's narrative content to its material form, the reader is able to enhance her semiotic understanding of its "meaning." She may be more abstractedly amused than ideologically concerned at this point by these received images and how they might inform her own experience. But there is still a "self" in her consciousness.

Or almost. It is about here that the speaker falls asleep.

The eye drops, weighted, through the lines
the burin made, the lines that move apart
like ripples above sand,
dispersing storms, God's spreading fingerprint,
and painfully, finally, that ignite
in watery prismatic white-and-blue. (*The Collected Poems* 57)

Just as the human figures disappear into the vague chronicles of "history and theology," so the textual figures fade into a further abstraction—in this case the ultimate abstraction. The speaker, now represented by a synecdochic "eye," "drops, weighted" in sleep, induced perhaps by the hypnotic toils of that "initial letter" or perhaps by sheer boredom with the unextraordinary coffee-table text.

Like Alice who falls asleep and into the story her sister is reading to her, an enormous shift in scale and perspective occurs as the speaker descends into the monstrous recesses of the engraved print, "through the lines / the burin made." The disembodied "eye" of the passive reader will become an active "I" in the second long section of the poem as the speaker begins her journey from reading a book to writing her own version, as well as becoming a character in that version. Like the opium-induced dreams of Coleridge in "Kubla Khan" or De Quincey in *Confessions of an English Opium-Eater*, the speaker's dream text will pick up where the alleged physical text left off and eventually rewrite or expand upon the Orientalist narrative therein. Bishop appeals to the trope of the dream-induced narrative and the safety it affords the writer to venture into dangerous or potentially scandalous material. But in this case the danger or scandal seems related to the perils of representation, particularly when it means conjuring up one's own life. We hope real experience will grant us more than the merely picturesque, more than a reduction of the world to caricatures of itself. We hope we can remember it as well as we lived it. We hope we lived it.

The cavernous lines of the text continue to assume new forms and now "move apart / like ripples above sand." The protean writing transforms itself into a string of associational likenesses, clauses that increase in dramatic stature as they recast the lines the burin made in other Middle Eastern dramas—now one of divine intervention. The "lines that move apart" are now "dispersing storms." The syntax has begun to twist out of comfortable linear shape. Subject complements become disconnected from their subjects, and verbs that have been relatively present disappear into the lofty but uncertain grammatical function of gerunds. And this little apocalypse in language reaches its climax when the omniscient source of all narrative finally appears. The orthographical marks are now "God's spreading fingerprint," the definitive typological interpretation of the world as God's text.

But because any interest in the literal relationship between worldly signs and their transcendental origins has proved unconvincing in the poem until now—monuments, remember, are tired—the dream of signification continues in surreal form until it erupts in a suitably fantastic display of fireworks and flood. We are uncertain what it is that happens "painfully," but we can locate parallel relative pronouns that help us: "The lines *that* move apart / like ripples above sand, / . . . and painfully, finally *that* ignite." The speaker suggests she physically feels the final destruction of this text, although "painfully" strikes us as one of Bishop's wonderful sudden lexical indulgences—as when going through her absent mother's things in "In the Village" she finds a "thick white teacup with a small red-and-blue butterfly on it, *painfully* desirable" (*The Collected Prose* 256). This pain may have something to do with the profane pleasure the speaker—like the child—experiences in the forbidden aesthetic, the figures that no longer represent anything readily accessible to the conscious "adult" mind.

The final image is as beautiful as it is destructive, and it is the first truly enigmatic moment in the poem—one that foreshadows the final scene. That which "ignite[s]" "painfully . . . in watery prismatic white-and-blue" is also perhaps "painfully desirable" in that it appears beyond the grasp of even the dreamer. Like Proteus, who if held fast by "strength and courage" can tell Menelaus about his journey and "the distances to be covered," text, if handled rightly, can offer the traveler meaningful information. If not, it can just as quickly transform itself into water and "blazing fire" (*The Odyssey* 72–74).

In the final refusal to make the perfect rhyme, the easy ordering of cultural experience that characterized the earlier text is further overturned. What could have been almost perfectly predictable trimeter lines made up of two dactylic feet and a final cretic foot, topped off with the strong masculine rhyme "that ignite . . . blue-and-white," is not. And the inversion, the willed imperfection, draws attention to itself. The serpentine "toiling" or coiling of the final sentence, which may have been rendered somewhat orderly by the final couplet, hints at that order and then turns it on its glib head. The hyphens that separate and bind the final psychedelic spectacle are not like Dickinson's but suggest her habit of endowing the dash with an odd power to mean. In this case the final white—the archetypal color of illumination—is instead a final watery blue, although "white-and-blue" are meant to be read as one, like waves. Like other final scenes in Bishop's poems, the sea is the sight of any "illumination" the poem may offer at this point.[1] But because "illumination" is always precarious business in her poems, not something doled out to every sailor who passes by, we will have to wait and trust in retroactive reading to make sense of what we have witnessed. What began as a tired, familiar text finishes much improved by this final prismatic dispersion of letters. And on these strange waters we drift off and into a new narrative—or at least a fresh attempt to inscribe the exotic.

III

After so much abstract activity comes a brief silence, the line break suggesting a pause to allow for scenery changes. Then, suddenly, the speaker appears to wake up to full daylight and consciousness. The mid-action, present progressive, however, quickly settles into the past tense of memory.

> Entering the Narrows at St. Johns
> the touching bleat of goats reached to the ship.
> We glimpsed them, reddish, leaping up the cliffs
> among the fog-soaked weeds and butter-and-eggs. (*The Collected Poems* 57–58)

The first thing we notice about this new version of the speaker's own travels is how animated and realistic the scene is compared to the lifeless, unreal poses the photographs offer. We see animals doing something in nature and weather. But we also notice the sentimental adjective "touching," which sends the wonderfully musical second line off on three frolicking trochees whose almost symmetrical inversion of phonemes "ch" and "t" (*touching bleat of goats reached*) gives phonetic spring to the guttural realism of *bleating goats*. Alexander Pope would have been charmed—but maybe a bit suspicious.

It is when the recollection pans through the "fog-soaked weeds" and settles on the "butter-and-eggs" in a brilliant and funny sylleptic slippage of language—"We glimpsed them . . . / among the fog-soaked weeds and butter-and-eggs"—that the parody reveals itself in sense as well as sound. Michael Riffaterre describes the syllepsis as a rhetorical device:

> [It is] the trope that consists in using one word with two mutually incompatible meanings without repeating that word. One word is acceptable in the context in which the word appears; the other meaning is valid only in the intertext to which the word also belongs and which it represents at the surface of the text as the tip of the intertextual iceberg. The syllepsis is a mere phonetic shape that is filled in turn by two otherwise alien universes of representation. (*Fictional Truth* 131)

As long as the goats are "glimpsed . . . among the fog-soaked weeds," everything is rather normal, the context being mimetically valid. It is when "butter-and-eggs" is introduced that the "intertextual iceberg" surfaces and signals a split in the speaker's consciousness. Whereas butter-and-eggs—also known as toadflax—is a common weed, it is also breakfast in America. And with this sylleptic slip we come to a certain realization, a certain trivialization of events. The scene has proved picturesque. The speaker's attempts at rewriting the experience of travel have not moved far beyond the emptied figures in the heavy book, and she seems to catch herself in the embarrassing act of being a passive observer, a tourist. The result is complex comedy. The playful last word, that self-conscious undermining of the falsely Romantic, parodies all that led up to it. We see a similar bathetic breakfast in "Arrival at Santos," the introductory poem to the later 1965 collection *Questions of Travel*:

> ... Oh, tourist,
> is this how this country is going to answer you
>
> and your immodest demands for a different world,
> and a better life, and complete comprehension
> of both at last, and immediately,
> after eighteen days of suspension?
>
> Finish your breakfast. . . . (*The Collected Poems* 89)

The sudden fall to earth, the intrusion of the quotidian into the rhapsodic, puts a similar self-mocking spin on the tourist's flight of fancy. Being "touched" by the Romantic rusticity of a landscape over breakfast suggests the same intellectual and emotional investment in the exotic that we witnessed in the case of the Arabs. And the passive, passing observation reintroduces the "intertextual iceberg" we witnessed in the first part of the poem. Clichéd Romantic narratives are recirculated when our reactions to foreign experience are underweighed and superficial.

But how much credit shall we give the speaker for this semiotic reading? The wavering of the poem's central intelligence is one of its fine points, perhaps its finest. The speaker's strange aptitude has what Gerard Genette in *Narrative Discourse* calls a paraleptic quality: she seems to be giving us more information than she realizes, and this becomes particularly apparent in the second part of the poem where each random detail the speaker marches out feels loaded with potential significance she does not acknowledge or pursue. Yet from time to time she seems to come to herself, sending momentary tremors through the surface narrative. And these sylleptic splits or slippages in the speaker's language and consciousness remain with us like echoes, affecting the way we read the rest of the poem. We, too, must do two things at once: we must pay heed to the referential meaning of the scenes and simultaneously remember that hermeneutic "intertextual iceberg" that floats beneath and supports them—the picturesque that seduces us when we are not looking.

IV

The scenes that follow rush past us with the speed of images flipped through in a travel magazine, although the idiosyncratic narration calls our attention to details and correspondences the "average" tourist might not notice or create.

And at St. Peter's the wind blew and the sun shone madly.
Rapidly, purposefully, the Collegians marched in lines,
crisscrossing the great square with black, like ants.
In Mexico the dead man lay
in a blue arcade; the dead volcanoes
glistened like Easter lilies.
The jukebox went on playing "Ay, Jalisco!"
And at Volubilis there were beautiful poppies
splitting the mosaics; the fat old guide made eyes. (*The Collected Poems*
58)

Narration seems almost incapable of keeping step with experience, or the memory of it. Having consumed such an abundance of visual and aural stimulation, the best the speaker can do is offer moments detached from linear time and space, each scene and figure a world unto itself in the vast bricolage that is her history. There is excitement in the varied rhythms, as if each town and country demands its own syncopated cadence. Direct experience proves much more vivid than the indirect experience of reading. In this pastiche of joyful color, even the dead are attractive.

In her book *Elizabeth Bishop: Restraints of Language*, C. K. Doreski argues that in this part of the poem human life proves historically linear and thus frustrates the "struggle to find a language willing to accommodate the traveler's fluid, trope-empowered knowledge" (7). Little in the speaker's experience abroad, or at least her memory of it, however, suggests historical linearity. And the frenetic, chaotic flood of images suggests a positive liberation from the trope-*impoverished* account of the foreign experience in the book she could not stay awake to read. As long as the speaker can identify her environment in terms of familiar cultural figures—the saints, "the Collegians," "Easter lilies"—she seems to be able to ground her subjects metaphorically. And with this confidence comes a versatility and expansiveness in language. The sacred dead, for example, do a haunting dance to the rhythmic phonic texture of the enjambed lines "In Mexico the dead man lay / in a blue arcade" as the iambic monosyllables strut and glide on a long a [e]. And it is easy to give oneself up to the melopoetics and rich animation of "at Volu*bilis* there were *beautiful poppies* / *splitting* the mo*saics*"—the sounds play off and upon each other like a Baroque quartet. It is an image both intellectually and aesthetically compelling. How wonderful to find nature one-upping art with such a sly, vainglorious trick.

If "the fat old guide" didn't "make eyes" and appear like a nasty little stain on the poem's elegant fabric, we would perhaps lose ourselves altogether in this imagistic celebration of the aesthetic Christian world. And as we move on to cooler climates and continue to enjoy the sensorial splendor and sudden odd drama, we begin to wonder just what we are to make of so many linguistic snapshots.

> In Dingle harbor a golden length of evening
> the rotting hulks held up their dripping plush.
> The Englishwoman poured tea, informing us
> that the Duchess was going to have a baby. (*The Collected Poems* 58)

There has been a certain aesthetic gluttony to the speaker's own wandering eye, and this last "Victorian" scene (tea and duchesses are too quaint to be taken completely seriously by anybody but the English in the twentieth century) puts a neat, prosaic, picturesque cap on the poem's most lyrical passage.[2] The echo of the earlier figure—"the grim lunette"—is slight, barely audible but nevertheless present. And the whirl of activity in the poem's last fifteen lines, with their emphasis on metaphor and their preference for scene over summary, will fail to sustain itself beyond the borders of the Christian empire.

> And in the brothels of Marrakesh
> the little pockmarked prostitutes
> balanced their tea-trays on their heads
> and did their belly-dances; flung themselves
> naked and giggling against our knees,
> asking for cigarettes. . . . (58)

The suddenly sensual ribaldry contrasts wildly with the Englishwoman pouring tea and the duchess with child, where sex seems as distant from conception as raw flax from fine linen. Belly dancers in a Marrakesh brothel is a mise-en-scène easily pulled from a novel by Flaubert or Nerval, except that the veils that stimulate desire by forestalling it are off.

Yet the freedom the speaker seems to have enjoyed in random recollection slowly stops with the return of the Oriental. She hesitates in the face of the familiar trope previously so emptied out that it faded into the scenery, taking the text with it. The language of metaphor that has helped inscribe scenes located somewhere in the Christian empire appears to lose its bearings in this exotic scenario. As Morocco comes back to her, it seems to require no aesthetic adornment beyond direct description.

These little giggling girls are nothing like the blooming vessels we come across in Romantic Orientalist fiction. They have physical flaws, and the only desire they manifest is for processed Western tobacco. And passion—that vague, desirable sensorial-intellectual complex—is supplanted by controlled alarm as the speaker watches an Oriental spectacle reenacted perhaps just for her. The prostitutes do not seem to belly dance spontaneously; rather, they "did *their* belly-dances": they perform the rituals that specifically identify them as exotic in the popular Occidental imagination—just as the guidebook said they would.

But in this usurpation of cultural narratives, who is reading whom? It is hard to say whether the speaker is scandalized by the fulfillment of her own Orientalist expectations—the girls *are* naked—or surprised by the human personalities that inhabit the living bodies. In either case, the objects of the Orientalist gaze, in spite of their subordinate position, seem to be having more fun than the voyeur. She is less confident now. She is out of her element.

This is not exactly the same scene Bishop describes for Marianne Moore in a letter from Morocco in 1936, but the prudence she uses when discussing "delicate" subjects with "Miss Moore"—a thoroughly modern artist but a rather Victorian woman—suggests the prudish response of the earlier speaker.

> The dancing is of course very improper but sometimes extremely
> amusing—as, for example, when the lady, to show how still she keeps
> the top of her head, dances with a tray on it, holding a teapot and
> glasses full of tea. Without spilling any she even lies down and rolls
> over, and at the end sits on the floor and takes a glass of tea off the tray
> and offers it to you, with her toes. (*One Art* 41)

The circus stunt would have appealed to Moore who shared with Bishop a delight in the extraordinary and strange. But in the poem, where the "improper dancing" gets more attention than the tea tray and prostitutes replace "the lady," there is the sense that something more unsavory than a circus is in town.

Earlier in the letter, Bishop describes the French "protectorate" that would be the site of much conflict between the Germans and the Allied forces during the war and would not regain its independence until 1956: "Morocco was so nice—in spite of the Moorish architecture, which is so awful, and the rather unfriendly atmosphere which had been caused by the French occupation (one immediately sympathizes with the Moors)—that we stayed probably longer than we should have" (*One Art* 40). The relationship between the foreign presence in the poem and the entertaining, supplicating "local color" is also unsettling. Something about moving away from the distancing comforts of the metaphorical and scenic and into direct interaction with people makes the speaker uneasy: "It was somewhere near there / I saw what frightened me most of all" (*The Collected Poems* 58).

This analeptic statement puts the Morocco experience into better focus: the speaker is no longer charmed by aesthetic landscape but is frightened by reality. Out of her element, she is unable to cope with experience for which she has no preexisting category. The move from reflective metaphor to direct statement signals a change in the speaker's attitude toward the subject. We understand now that this attitude is a reflection of fear—fear of the truly foreign, the unknown.

Like an occupied territory, the poem's representational landscape continues to be disturbed by native insurgence that strikes at something vital to the speaker's system of identification and destabilizes her narrative control over the subject. The result is not sympathy (Bishop's own response to the tensions in Morocco) but increased fear. And now the poem's mood mutates even more dramatically toward the macabre as the speaker finally confronts the supreme physical embodiment of the emptied sign:

> A holy grave, not looking particularly holy,
> one of a group under a keyhole-arched stone baldaquin
> open to every wind from the pink desert.
> An open, gritty, marble trough, carved solid
> with exhortation, yellowed
> as scattered cattle-teeth;
> half-filled with dust, not even the dust
> of the poor prophet paynim who once lay there.
> In a smart burnoose Khadour looked on amused. (58)

What promises to be holy, thus an invulnerable depository for our hopes and dreams of the transcendental, decays when exposed to the elements. The shock of the physical reality once again destroys the speaker's expectations. In the grave the speaker witnesses a complex interpenetration of the ravages of time and history the ubiquitous book of lifeless photos cannot begin to communicate. Nothing the book said prepared her for her aversion to the physical thing itself, the emptiness of what should have been full.

"[C]arved solid with exhortation," the grave's intended function was rhetorical as well as physical—it was meant to incite, encourage, lecture the living, and house the dead. As an active sign, an interlocutor between the material world of bodies and the immaterial world of ideas, it was meant to communicate in the fullest possible sense. But now, in the eyes of the troubled tourist, the grave appears nothing more than defunct architecture, an empty signifier. An "open, gritty, marble trough," its function concerns livestock rather than men, and in a wonderful shift of connotative vehicle—one highly abstract, "exhortation"; the other lowly and concrete, "scattered cattle-teeth"—the shapes carved to serve the purposes of religion resemble the molars of dead, domestic beasts. The tenor, the grave itself, is usurped by its own vehicle—"scattered cattle-teeth"—and all metaphorical potential beyond the merely descriptive is dead.

The holy remains of the pagan priest, "the poor prophet paynim," turn out to be literal desert dust. The visit is a bust, and the voyage was probably long, hot, and generally uncomfortable. But there is something more disturbed than the mere physical in the final lines of the poem's middle section. The familiar metaphor "dust to dust," one we use casually and claim to comprehend, is defamiliarized in this alien context. The speaker is frightened by what she sees in this landscape, which demands too much from her—a landscape that seems to ask her to reconsider what knowledge she has about mortality even as it appears to say nothing. This is not sublime terror in the face of the unknown, something Baudelaire would conjure. It is more bald astonishment at the signifying potential of the empty desert grave. It is not empty; she simply cannot read it.

Khadour seems to know something she does not. While the tourist struggles with herself in the foreign world he has guided her to, he "looked on amused." He is hardly Virgil, every traveler's dream guide. Khadour's ironic expression contrasts greatly with the speaker's furrowed brow, and his confident humor parodies her own previously superior sentiments when she felt in charge of herself and the language she used to inscribe the environment. In his "smart burnoose," a terrific choice of adjectives—Westerners would hardly qualify the long, loose-flowing cloak of desert dwellers as "smart"—he stands apart. He has a name, and he is not particularly sympathetic to the tourist and her interpretive struggles with shrines. Like the language used to describe him, the suddenly alliterative line with its internal off-rhymes—"In a *smart* burn*oose* Khadour looked on *amused*"—he is self-contained, a lyrical finale to what has become a disturbingly unaccommodating narrative.

V

After another pause signaled by a double line break, the speaker comes to. But when her consciousness is relocated in the poem's original present tense, the phlegmatic attitude toward the text returns. The "I" that has been guiding the personal narrative and that had replaced the "eye" of the passive reader has proven equally unsatisfactory to the traveler. And now the texts— the speaker's narrative, the illustrated book of Wonders, the Bible—merge in the ambiguous determiner that launches the poem's conclusion: "Everything only connected by 'and' and 'and.' Open the book. (The gilt rubs off the edges of the pages and pollinates the fingertips.) Open the heavy book" (58).

The proximity principle does not apply in this final concordance of texts: "everything" fails to move beyond rhetorical contingency. The paratactic narration of events, the reeling in of so many disconnected impressions, has failed to give these events the force and immediacy the speaker had hoped for. Her modern method has proved no more effective than the rationally organized discourse of the heavy picture book. And with its reverberations of Old Testament discourse, "*only* connected by 'and' and 'and,'" her own book seems to level rather than illuminate experience.

Redirected to the speaker's act of reading, "Open the book," we understand the mimetic reference and return to the first "heavy book" in the poem. If the text appeared to disintegrate in the earlier stanza to make way for the speaker's dream-text, the book continues to anatomize in a parody of that earlier moment. But the apocalyptic splendor of the "sand" and the "fingerprints" in stanza one is muted and domesticated when echoed in "gilt" and "fingertips." Yet embedded in this aside, which indulges in the texture of descriptive surfaces even as it suggests their ephemerality ("The gilt rubs off the edges / of the pages and pollinates the fingertips"), a phonetic pun hides like a reluctant ghost. There is a sense of "guilt" that, like "gilt," bleeds off the pages and onto the speaker's hands. She has been unable to move beyond its images because the cultural iconography she locates there is also engraved in her own text.

Returning to the failed text with insistent definite pronouns, "*the* book," "*the* heavy book," the speaker admits its primacy. Having failed to pursue her own experiences in language, settling on a barrage of paratactic observations that resolved like the "toils of an initial letter" in their own aesthetic singularities; having been unable to do much more than gape—literally—at the naked dancing girls whose Orientalist parody seems to supersede her own in writing; having been unable to read the desert landscape in terms available to her, the speaker returns dejected and even hostile to the original text. "The book" has proven to contain the cultural narratives that inform all her texts, particularly their limitations—because when its metanarratives have failed, so has she.

VI

If until now the speaker's intelligence has appeared to waver between paralepsis and self-consciousness, between hermeneutic limitation and the hermeneutic agility necessary for the kind of ironic distance that, for example, precipitates syllepsis, the final scene settles this uncertainty. The knowledge the speaker leaves us with, however, can only be considered in terms of a dialectical resolution. As the speaker's diction plunges into the nether regions of American argot, she highlights—in tawdry neon—one sad fact of cultural tourism. Something we now know she knows: "Open the heavy book. Why couldn't we have seen / this old Nativity scene while we were at it" (58).

In this sudden colloquialism, which reduces action to an afterthought or a by-product, all the poem's activity threatens to dissolve into the "it" that clinches the verb phrase. And with this final self-effacement, the speaker implicates herself in the dumb arrogance that feeds on supreme fictions like so many herds of cultivated cattle. Because as soon as we assume that these narratives are "vast and obvious" rather than complex and problematic and thus worthy of serious attention, we corroborate our inability to live or read or speak beyond the perimeters or limitations of cultural representation.

Yet this yoking of slang and the sacrosanct suggests a resistance on the speaker's part. She knows where she has been, and she's worried about it. Her own travel narrative threatens to recirculate the kind of reel-to-reel (or, in more contemporary terms, "sound bite") vision that is the result of a consumerist approach to the world's cultural markets. Through the speaker and particularly her responses to the Oriental, Bishop is exploring the search for sympathy in language—sympathy that will open up the living reality of the foreign or "exotic" rather than shut it down or confine it within the limitations of her own culture's restrictive narratives. But like all of Bishop's quests, she avoids epic resolve in favor of a more precarious lyrical uncertainty. If pure vision is never possible, if we must always regard our experience through the lens of our cultural inheritance, the least we can do is remain aware of this latter fact by imposing the self on the consciousness of it.

The final scene is a rewriting of "this old Nativity." It is an attempt not to resurrect its Christian significance but rather to defamiliarize it to the point where its enigmatic potential becomes relevant. Putting this scene in sequential context with the rest of the stanza, however, reminds us that Bishop is no preacher with a message, yet she is still a crafty defender of the obscure. And once again her abrupt revelations, if we can call them that, materialize when least expected.

> Everything only connected by "and" and "and."
> Open the book. (The gilt rubs off the edges
> of the pages and pollinates the fingertips.)
> Open the heavy book. Why couldn't we have seen
> this old Nativity scene while we were at it?
> —the dark ajar, the rocks breaking with light,
> an undisturbed, unbreathing flame,
> colorless, sparkless, freely fed on straw,
> and, lulled within, a family with pets,
> —and looked and looked our infant sight away. (58–59)

This is an indefinite although definitely climactic ending to a poem that has been struggling with the hermeneutic limitations and potential of the unknown. Yet it is precisely because of this struggle that the final spectacle feels earned. If we do not take the entire poem into account, it would be easy to consider this Blakean ending a nostalgic lament for the purer vision of preconceptual infancy. But the speaker has proved herself too savvy for such Romantic despair. Ashbery said this of the ending of "2,000 Illustrations": "I am unable to exhaust the meaning and mysteries of its concluding line . . . and I suspect that its secret has very much to do with the nature of Miss Bishop's poetry. Looking, or attention, will absorb the object with its meaning" (*New York Times Book Review* 8). The nature of the speaker's attention has suddenly changed, as if she has come to some understanding about how interpretation depends on the eye in ways she had only dreamed of. And something in the ordinary depiction of the Nativity seems to spark this vague knowledge in her.

When the speaker takes in the final, tired reproduction, something happens to her that goes beyond the automatic reaction "calendar art" normally inspires. She seems to recognize some intrinsic value in the emptying out of these icons. And pushing this representational tactic further, she continues erasing what vital signs rest in the images through a series of linguistic negations—"un" prefixes and "less" suffixes. The holy family in a manger, now simply "a family with pets," is emptied as a sign, stripped of its overfamiliar identity, its cultural baggage. And in this partial parody of the processes of representation, she reduces and isolates the figures yet does not posit alternative meanings, replace the unknown with the known, or assign tropes. Having feared and failed to read her experiences, she chooses to start again, from nothing, with the simple knowledge that she knows nothing.

In this final complication of the speaker's paraleptic knowledge, she forces us to reexamine our own arrogance as readers—are we so sure we know more than she is capable of telling us? Perhaps we have been duped by her self-effacement all along. Are we tourists, consuming images, reflecting on a bit of culture "while we're at it"? She has learned something about the shortcomings of available epistemological definitions, which assign sight either to the rational (Classicist) or to the pre-rational (Romantic). She has seen that this is hardly what happens when Occidental man is faced with the Oriental other. And in an overturning of such categories of knowledge, she chooses to replace the unconscious eye of the adult with the self-conscious eye of the infant. We are not prepared to think in fresh, nonprescriptive ways about what we are seeing. We must therefore seize this knowledge and begin our journey again.

Like the earlier engraved lines that "ignite" as they dissolve, the rocks "breaking with light" emit a paradoxical flame. There is a Heraclitian quality to each suspended adjective that contains dynamic verb roots—"disturb," "breath," "color," "spark"—even as each is denied a life force. The language is simultaneously dead and alive. Thus just at the point when the sign appears to be utterly dissembled—like the earlier text in the dream or the tomb in the desert—there comes a surge in signification that, however unavailable to the speaker, nevertheless sparks a change in her consciousness. Such is the stuff of enigmas: the residual phenomena that remain to be explained after the effects of known causes are subtracted; the physical world becoming clearer at the moment it is least available to us through existent conceptual modes. The final flame, "unbreathing," "sparkless," neither reflects nor emits light; it is self-generating and perhaps has nothing to say to us that we can ever understand, given our limited cultural schemata. But its very opacity is painfully desirable. Children understand this. So does the traveler who, like Bishop, reads the world fully aware that it may not speak in a tongue she will comprehend. There is no such thing as complete concordance. That is the beauty of it and the terms of traveling right.

"Questions of Travel"

LESSONS IN HISTORY, TOLERANCE, AND THE ART OF BEING IN UNCERTAINTIES

"Notre nature est dans le mouvement;
le repos entier est la mort."

—PASCAL

I

WISHING TO ESCAPE THE DEBILITATING LONELINESS OF NEW YORK IN 1951, Bishop at the age of forty decided to take a trip around the world. When the proposed trip was suddenly cancelled because of overbooking just as she was preparing to leave, Bishop reportedly asked, "Well, where do you have boats going?" When she was told South America, she replied, "All right, I'll come on that one." Thus rerouted *par hazard,* or by an accident of history, she arrived in Brazil—hardly the weighing of choices one anticipates with fateful decisions (Fountain and Brazeau 126). She would be nursed through Christmas by her future mate, Lota de Macedo Soares, after suffering a violent allergic reaction while visiting Rio de Janeiro. Overwhelmed by the attention and generosity of her hosts and drawn to the satisfying eccentricities of the landscape, Bishop would fall in love with Brazil; and what was to have been a brief stopover lasted fifteen years. Within the first month of her visit she writes to Marianne Moore, indulging in the excitement they both shared as "literalists of the imagination" in the "always more successful surrealism of everyday," particularly in the natural world (Kalstone, *Becoming a Poet* 15).

There are so many things here you would like; I have written you so
many imaginary letters and bored you to death with descriptive
conversation many times. I have been staying mostly at my friend Lota's
country place in Petrópolis, about 40 miles from Rio, and it is a sort of
dream-combination of plant & animal life. I really can't believe it at
all. Not only are there highly impractical mountains all around with
clouds floating in & out of one's bedroom, but waterfalls, orchids, all
the Key West flowers I know & Northern apples and pears as well. Lota
has sold one of her places to a famous Polish zoo man and you just have
to drive down the mountainside for two minutes to see a black jaguar, a
camel, all the most beautiful birds in the world. I think of you every
minute there. The zoo man—I can't believe this yet myself, and we
have no common language even—gave me a TOUCAN for my birthday,
the other day. . . . I can't imagine anything nicer than to have you in
Brazil, too. I'm afraid I'm a real "literalist"—I have to have a real
toucan, and then I can't even do him justice. (*One Art* 236)

Moore's foreign existence at home—her immediate world was always an
exotic place—made her limited experience abroad immaterial to her appreciation of Bishop's travel experiences. "There's no way of telling what really
is 'experience' anyway, it seems to me. Look at what Miss Moore has done
with what would seem to me like almost none," Bishop notes to May Swenson
in 1958 (*One Art* 360). Bishop's letters to Moore about Brazilian customs
and landscape come close in tone and tenor to the *Brazil* poems in her 1965
collection *Questions of Travel*. They are playful and always pleasantly aston-
ished at the natural capacity of places and people to confound the logical
expectations of the northern visitor.

Rio de Janeiro, Samambaia near Petrópolis, and Ouro Prêto would be
homes to Bishop like none since her early childhood in Nova Scotia with
her maternal grandparents; and she would never re-create or replace them
on the North American continent. The accidental voyage and the dramatic
reversal—from initial violent reaction to real veneration—are apt models
for poems that question the intentions and fate of the itinerant lifestyle
because the questions, like the answers, must make room for the inconclusive hazards and happiness that characterize any life, but particularly the
life abroad.

II

Bishop's poem "Questions of Travel" addresses the dubiety that plagues or
graces self-imposed exile where so much depends on how completely one
can apply Keats's notion of "Negative Capability" to one's own existence:
"That is when a man is capable of being in uncertainties, Mysteries, doubts,

without any irritable reaching after fact and reason." Accepting this as a personal philosophy, however, means never going back to that relative concept we call home. And while most people will pack that seat of fact and reason along with them in theory—we cannot help but take first causes personally—some will leave it behind. The decision is never free, Bishop will tell us. But to come to this inevitability, the poem will first chart the tug and pull between uncertainty and reason, the attraction to the impenetrable that resides in the mysterious interstices of another culture, and the cautionary voice that warns us away.

She will also offer us not so much a lesson in history as a way to read history in the empirical data foreign travel offers us. Our capacity for empathy is proportionate to our desire to read or interpret the most insignificant details a place might offer. And uncertainty can lead to knowledge when the traveler looks at the particulars of the world with the subtle eye of a would-be artist. Aesthetics in this sense can contribute to the public interest, and the speaker will show us that curiosity is never idle when it reveals to us something about our own responsibilities as a nation.

The poem begins in protest. Excessive, exaggerated, the lush, wet Brazilian landscape overwhelms the speaker's senses and her definitions of nature's reasonable limitations. "The scenery," as Bishop notes wryly and repeatedly in letters, "is unbelievably impractical."

> There are too many waterfalls here; the crowded streams
> hurry too rapidly down to the sea,
> and the pressure of so many clouds on the mountaintops
> makes them spill over the sides in soft slow-motion,
> turning to waterfalls under our very eyes.
>
> —For if those streaks, those mile-long, shiny, tearstains
> aren't waterfalls yet,
> in a quick age or so, as ages go here,
> they probably will be.
> But if the streams and clouds keep travelling, travelling,
> the mountains look like hulls of capsized ships,
> slime-hung and barnacled. (*The Collected Poems* 93)

The language is almost prosaic, the objections almost pure panic. But there are subtle linguistic indulgences, small poetic excesses that pepper the prose and idle the lament, making it something of a song. A ground rhythm is established right away by dactyls that tumble on like the water they inflect, although they are occasional, often interrupted. Compound nouns repeat and exaggerate this effect—"wa-ter-falls," "moun-tain-tops"—while other key trisyllabic terms repeat and reinforce the movement, "travelling, travelling," or oppose it, "barnacled." We are reminded of Bishop's reflection on a similar melopoetic pleasure in her short prose piece "Gwendolyn": "In the first place, her beautiful name. Its dactyl trisyllables could have gone on forever as far as I was concerned" (*Collected Prose* 216). Like the child responding to the music in a name, the speaker is enjoying the rhythms all this natural chaos embodies or inspires. We suspect she would prefer that the lyrical flow would go on forever.

She appears captivated. There is something magical here—streams turn into waterfalls "under our very eyes." Even the final metaphor that almost arrests the water's movement as it stalls and capsizes the stanza echoes the three-beat thunder in its crustaceous final clinging. These poetic indulgences in what is otherwise a perfectly reasonable prose attract attention to themselves and encourage us to identify the play of language with something other than the surface objections. The speaker's reaction, part resistance, part indulgence, is a presentation of a problem—a rather wonderful problem. We will understand after we have read the entire poem that this opening stanza suggests a traditional lyrical complaint. It is a call for guidance, although in this case earthly rather than divine. The speaker has doubts about her wanderlust, the value of her "worldly desires." And she will search her personal as well as her historical conscience for answers to the questions of travel that pursue her and threaten to send her packing once again.

The subject of the complaint extends beyond the love of another to the love of otherness—something the speaker feels intuitively drawn to against the "better" judgments instilled in her by her training. Bishop herself found in Brazil the kind of complex socioeconomic and racial mix, and subsequent kinetic cultural energy, that appeal to the more responsive imagination and the less invested nationalism. Reservations expressed by North American and British friends suggest that they did not share her enthusiasm for the southern continent. And their comments are important when taken as an indication of a pervasive attitude vis-à-vis the Latin countries Bishop addresses indirectly in "Questions of Travel." Ashley Brown, a close friend and writer, describes Bishop's attraction in equivocal terms: "There's something sort of anarchistic, something rather bizarre and surrealistic, about life in Brazil [that appealed to Elizabeth]" (Fountain and Brazeau 191). Although we suspect that Brown himself finds these alternative "states" interesting to visit, we sense he would not choose to live in them for an extended period.

In a 1991 article in *Partisan Review*, Pearl Bell, another friend, still finds Bishop's enthusiastic reaction to Brazilian life difficult to fathom even after forty years:

When Elizabeth told me she was going to stay in Brazil, I was puzzled and more than a little apprehensive. . . . I longed to be away from the suffocating heat, the bad food . . . the ubiquitous lassitude and incompetence, the unsettling sense of a world falling apart. . . . I did not find Rio exotic. . . . During the four convulsive days of Carnival, the entire country goes berserk, and the very air turns loud and wild. . . . I soon found the unceasing racket unbearable, the pounding beat of orgiastic delirium, the deafening, day-long niggling commotion, the samba-ing crowds in the streets—and fled to an apartment in Ipanema, where I reached for the most northernly book I could find—Harold Nicolson's *Some People*—seeking relief in his calm British prose from the wild clamor outside. (33)

There is little Bishop irony here. The gap between what Bishop saw and what some of her northern friends did not see is significant. It also helps us understand whom and what the poem is an answer to.

Bishop preferred the samba to the bossa nova, loved Carnival, and felt more at ease in the "orgiastic delirium" than she would later in the hallowed halls of Harvard. She would have more problems attempting to live in Ouro Prêto alone after Lota's death, but while she remained in "indigenous" circles she enjoyed the best years of her life. Whereas Brown confesses that "to keep one's head" one would have to become "a complete nominalist" to live in Brazil, he admires Bishop's capacity for being in uncertainties: "Elizabeth seemed perfectly in harmony with this barrage of sights, sounds, and smells that awaited one at every hand" (Schwartz and Estess 223).

The biographical fact of Bishop's attachment to and prolonged integration into Brazilian culture creates an interesting backdrop for a poem exploring the uncertainties, mysteries, and doubts of "being" in unfamiliar territory. Conscious of the questionable implications of cultural tourism, Bishop creates a first-person narrative voice that is not at all certain about her choices or her rights to such freedom. Why should she move around the world like a self-indulgent child, amusing herself with the realities of others—especially while serious, real work is being done at home? Yet in the course of the poem the speaker complicates conventional distinctions between the traveler as privileged observer and the target culture as observed object. We are asked to consider just what "home" means in a twentieth-century postcolonial context, what lessons there may be in tracing the steps of conquerors.

The poem's next stanza offers a litany of similar nervous questions. After so many superlatives—"too many waterfalls," "so many clouds"—we might ask, excessive in comparison with what? And the inevitable answer surfaces directly: home—that point of intellectual and cultural reference through which all other experience is filtered and gauged.

Think of the long trip home.
Should we have stayed at home and thought of here?
Where should we be today?
Is it right to be watching strangers in a play
in this strangest of theatres? (*The Collected Poems* 93)

Each question anticipates a problem in its own right, as if the speaker wishes to preempt all accusations by confessing first. She knows what old judgments will be passed and imagines new, more interesting ones. Having caught herself momentarily seduced by the lyrical landscape of the initial stanza, however, the speaker now switches to a stricter prose—"Think of the long trip home"—as well as a sudden formal perfect rhyme "today/play," as if waking from an imaginary, foreign dream of immersion into the daylight of rational consciousness, or home, which insists on distinctions and distances between "here and there."

In the tension created by the indecisive conditional tense and controlled iambs of the first and, eventually, the last lines of the stanza, we hear echoes—rhetorical and thematic—of Prufrock's near-crippling self-debate: "Should we have stayed at home . . . Oh must we dream our dreams?" Similarly, such self-conscious self-questioning threatens to undermine any confidence the speaker may have in her ability to interact with this new environment, leaving her passive and impotent in the face of so much beauty and potential for exploration beyond the confines of home or the self. And as the following question moves beyond the limits of conventional wisdom and into the ethics of intercultural relations, Bishop's speaker—like Eliot's Prufrock—exposes her implication in the cultural narratives that isolate her from the world turning beyond her immediate culture: "Is it right to be watching strangers in a play / in this strangest of theatres?"

If Prufrock is menaced by the bourgeois existence in which he plays a dull, although inextricable, role, the speaker in "Questions of Travel" is also haunted by the very language she uses in describing her position as a spectator rather than a player. With a play on the word *strange* from the Latin *extraneus*, meaning "external," "foreign," "outside," she reinforces the tendency of the tourist to equate "strangers" or foreigners with what is external to conceptions of the real—a tendency the speaker fears she may share. Underscoring this etymological pun with the theatre metaphor, the speaker underscores a subtle form of ethnocentrism not exclusive to "developed" countries but one that has important ramifications when certain nations hold inordinate sway over the world stage.

By limiting the representation of "others" to the derogatory status of "strange," we limit our own possibility for identification and thus cloister ourselves within the confines of our own cultural frontiers. But the question is double-edged. If the speaker exposes the exclusionism inscribed in the very language we use to talk about "strangers," she simultaneously questions it; she asks if it is right. Uneasy with the idea of being the privileged observer and self-conscious about becoming the controlling subject of her own narrative, the speaker questions her right to be an eyewitness. Isolated within our cultural prejudices, how can we presume?

Such social-scientific logic, however, threatens to kill the poem mid-stanza: How are we to live, let alone write, under the weight of so much inscrutable knowledge? And as the frenzied questions continue, the speaker adopts the subject position of a child, as if acknowledging the inevitable association. She will then use this point of view to create an imaginative counterforce, as Wallace Stevens suggests in "The Noble Rider and the Sound of Words," against the rational harassment of the parent.

The speaker's attraction to the South American continent is given further rhetorical reign as she assumes the epithet she ascribes herself.

> What childishness is it that while there's a breath of life
> in our bodies, we are determined to rush
> to see the sun the other way around?
> The tiniest green hummingbird in the world?
> To stare at some inexplicable old stonework,
> inexplicable and impenetrable,
> at any view,
> instantly seen and always, always delightful? (*The Collected Poems* 93)

There is a sudden rhetorical expansiveness, each incomplete sentence hinging on a determination "to rush" or "to rush to see." Things, a "hummingbird," "old stonework," break loose syntactically and contextually—not, as Fredric Jameson might argue, to be dislodged from the world and naturalized in an elitist, autonomous space but so they may be delivered from rational reification by the northern tourist.[1]

It is the stammering, visionary child, for whom so much is gladly impenetrable, who offers the speaker a way to read this new world. Reflection in the tranquillity of home or complete syntactical structures will not be what helps provide answers to her questions of travel; rather, it seems it will be in the breathless excitement of tactile immediacy. In this repetition of clauses and exuberant insistence on "inexplicable" and "always," the speaker acknowledges the impossibility of complete rational understanding. This means she cannot only momentarily forget herself in the admiration of the exotic object, but she can avoid the kind of cultural appropriation and reduction that occur when we insist things speak to us in languages we understand.

But all this unself-conscious, "childish" delight in the aesthetics of nature and stone craft comes not without reservations as the stanza terminates playfully on a note of satiation.

> Oh, must we dream our dreams
> and have them too?
> And have we room
> for one more folded sunset, still quite warm? (93)

The Brazilian landscapes become associated with food—"have our cake and eat it too," the sunset a hot-cross bun and not the first, straight out of the warm oven. And there is a suggestion in this final sigh of pleasure that there may be something sinful in all this aesthetic gluttony. Too much of any good thing cannot possibly be good for us, we are reminded in the nursery-rhyme morality of the intended pun. But the speaker will insist, in spite of the internalized voice that means to take her home to safety and a balanced diet.

III

In the next long stanza the speaker continues to dream her dreams "and have them too" by insisting that just as there is imaginative appeal in the clearest empirical data, so might there be latent historical import in the odd aesthetic detail.

> But surely it would have been a pity
> not to have seen the trees along this road,
> really exaggerated in their beauty;
> not to have seen them gesturing
> like noble pantomimists, robed in pink. (93–94)

Using lofty, psychedelic language reminiscent of that used by Stevens, Bishop animates her Brazilian landscape with an odd mélange of figures and colors—"exaggerated," "noble," "philosophical," and "pink"—qualities that do not gel in any logical way. But it is from here that she will embark on an odd lesson in history.

In 1961 Bishop was asked to write a book on Brazil for the *Time-Life* World Library Series, and this kind of studied fusion of incongruent qualities and detail would characterize her narration. The book project would be a battle with the editors from beginning to end, however, with only the first and eighth chapters retaining anything of Bishop's voice. Complaints to friends highlight the leveling of personality and language that often characterizes popular journalism's treatment of the "developing world" when sales take precedence over representational integrity.

No use the Flaubert stuff (although I CAN'T seem to compose any other way) since they will just put it through their own meat grinder, lawfully, and it will come out sounding like them no matter what I say. . . . And the worst is really that, like publishers, they keep paying lip service to "distinguished writing," "your own opinions," "your fine reputation," and blah blah blah—lying like RUGS. . . . [T]he Life editor wrote me that "you'd be surprised how much help an *outline* is," also, "although it may seem like a burden" . . . (on and on) a bibliography of the books I'm using "would be a good idea."—Teach your grandmother to suck eggs, please. They are INCREDIBLE, that's all. It is more like manufacturing synthetic whipped creme out of the by-products of a plastic factory than anything remotely connected with writing. (*One Art* 399–400)

What could easily be construed as the capricious rantings of an artist's wounded ego (and surely this was the word at *Time-Life*) might also be read as a hilarious and spirited rejection of the kind of consumerist approach to language and culture that characterizes those publications aiming for middle-class appeal.

Bishop's protest also attests to the fact that not only do aesthetics contribute to the public interest but political history is well served when it is simultaneously a subject of art. Bishop's lessons in history are usually overlooked by readers, except on those rare occasions when she has sent critics scrambling by referring to poems in explicitly "political" terms (i.e., "Miracle for Breakfast" as her "Depression" poem or "From Trollope's Journal" as her "anti-Eisenhower" poem) (*One Art* 439). Because she avoided overt public activism in her poetry and life, many have assumed it did not exist. Bishop's struggle with the editors of *Time-Life*, however, reflects her dissatisfaction with the notion that the representation of a foreign culture should be honed to the expectations or tastes of an audience more interested in diversion than in real knowledge:

This awful optimism—this "up-beat," as he called it. . . . No one seems to see how damned condescending it is to think that Brazilians *like* "crazy" people like Kubitschek—or that a little corruption—or a *lot*—is good for South American countries. . . . The real trouble is going to be in New York—when they present me with their "up-beat" statistics to show that everything is wonderful and getting better and better, etc. . . . Maybe I can at least be *objective*, it will be no place to be critical, I know, but surely I don't have to say that Brasilia, for one example, is absolutely perfect. . . . If only I don't end up writing the way they talk. (Bishop in Bell 49)

Bishop's complaints are interesting not only because they reveal a far more political personality than has generally been suspected but also because they point to the degree to which she trusted in aesthetics to undermine cultural types. Taking Ginsberg's "brilliant" question personally—"Are you going to let your emotional life be run by TIME magazine?"—Bishop insists that political acumen and rhetorical integrity are not distinct divisions of labor but inextricably bound and dependent on one another for the fuller realization of each.

The difference between the two chapters in which Bishop's idiolect rings clear and the rest of the book in which her voice disappears into the innocuous recesses of the sociolect is dramatic. What Bishop's chapters do and what *Time-Life* did not want (they preferred "those false, let's-face-it, summing-up cracks") is to focus on the illogical, self-contradictory character of Brazil as a nation and then celebrate this as a form of social welfare in prose that rises to the occasion (*One Art* 406). Featuring Bishop—a "real" writer as writer—proved once again, in the case of *Time-Life*, more a marketing gimmick than a genuine attempt at a marriage of "art" and mass media. Ford Motor Company had experienced similar difficulties with Marianne Moore, whom they had engaged to name their "state of the art" model in 1958. And when, after much exasperating debate, they settled on "the Edsel" rather than Moore's "Armadillo" (if anything, more anatomically accurate), many would agree that the name for the highly unsuccessful model was part of the problem.

IV

The title of the introductory chapter to the *Time-Life* text, "A Warm and Reasonable People," was most likely borrowed from the ministry of tourism rather than concocted by Bishop. Most of the chapter is pure Bishop, however, much in the way the central section of the poem "Questions of Travel" is. The narrative trajectory resembles less linear flight than a series of subject-to-subject foragings that feel like digressions rather than logical inductions or deductions. These digressions tend to take the form of anecdotes, much as we find in what she referred to as the "prose-poetry" of "In the Village." Connections between subjects are difficult to explain rationally and are better recognized instinctively or through slow, sustained, conscious examination. But, as is usual in Bishop's poetry and prose, the sudden switches are not gratuitous; they do not jar. Rather, they surprise.

Speaking of "natural responsibility" and social relations in Brazil, Bishop emphasizes the role of tolerance, pinpointing cultural practices she knows will shock a more prudish North American sensibility.

Home and family are very important in Brazil. But because there is no divorce, strange situations arise: second and third "marriages," unrecognized legally but socially accepted, in which there are oddly mixed sets of children. These situations merely give the Brazilians a chance to exercise their unique talent for kindly tolerance. In fact, in the spirit of mollification the courts more than two decades ago ruled that henceforth no one could be legally termed illegitimate. (*Brazil* 13)

Nipping conventional morality at the bud of its sexual inhibitions and attendant legal system, Bishop sees a superior humanity in Brazilians' "looser" domestic norms. During these rare intervals in the *Time-Life* text in which Bishop is given free rein, she often holds America up as a foil to Brazilian culture. Without being particularly obvious, however, she will consistently ask that same audience to reconsider its own democratic pretenses. The fact that no one may be "legally termed illegitimate" comes on the heels of a larger discussion of class relations in Brazil in which Bishop uses the same sort of comparative grammatical relations we see in the second stanza of "Questions of Travel." "Natural responsibility" and class relations in Brazil are indicative of "the *more* difficult and somewhat *broader* conceptions of what democracy generally means today"—"today" meaning a North America that tends to universalize time and space according to its own geographical particulars (*Brazil* 13).

The paragraph immediately following the "aside" concerning the legal status of all human beings born into this world puts a further spin on the subject of legitimacy. And the odd juxtaposition of a seemingly incompatible anecdote makes us search for connections between social tolerance and individual forbearance where we might not normally look for them.

There is a story about Rio de Janeiro and its beloved, decrepit *bondes* or open trolley cars. A *bonde* was careening along, overcrowded as usual, with men hanging to the sides like a swarm of bees. It barely stopped for a tall, gangling man to get off; and as he jumped from the step he fell, landing in a humiliating heap. His fellow passengers laughed. He pulled himself together, got up and with great dignity shouted after them: "Everyone descends from the *bonde* in the way he wants to."

That is the perfect statement of the Brazilian belief in tolerance and forbearance: everyone should be allowed to descend from the *bonde* in his or her own way. (*Brazil* 13)

These two paragraphs and the concluding "moral" make up the kind of surreal marriage of farce and social commentary we associate with the Chaplinesque. As Hart Crane notes in his poem of that name, "[T]hese fine collapses are not lies / more than pirouettes of any pliant cane" but the embodiments of general human strengths or weaknesses that more often than not are the direct result of social conditions (1226). Bishop was out to educate her audience, albeit in her nondidactic, subtle fashion. There were "lessons," strange and vital, to be learned in daily foreign dramas that could be instructive to that part of the world that defines itself as "developed."

Interviewed by Ashley Brown in Petrópolis in 1966, Bishop was asked if, as far as her poetry was concerned, she had "been able to get anything from Brazil except its appearances":

> Living the way I have happened to live here, knowing Brazilians, has made a great difference. The general life I have known here has of course had an impact on me. I think I've learned a great deal. Most New York intellectuals' ideas about "underdeveloped countries" are partly mistaken, and living among people of a completely different culture has changed a lot of my stereotyped ideas. (Schwartz and Estess 290)

Thus what could strike the Anglo tourist in the "uninterpreted" *bonde* scene above—or in Brazilian life in general—as yet another example of "ubiquitous lassitude and incompetence" or give one "the unsettling sense of a world falling apart" may well be a more complex or, as Bishop says, "broader conception of what democracy generally means today." One way to learn these things is in the actual living among "others," something Bishop insists influenced her poetry by changing her preconceived notions of the "underdeveloped" world. Direct contact with the "outside" may, however, inspire empathy only in those cases where the subject is as prepared to forgo her own deep-rooted cultural assumptions as she is able to ponder, if only inconclusively, the lessons of others.

V

Stanza three of "Questions of Travel" takes these matters of empathy to broader historical lengths. It is concerned with the material vestiges of colonialism and thus explores further the political implications of foreign travel. Stylistically similar to the *Brazil* chapters, the scene appears like an offbeat, playful anecdote. Yet here, too, we note the signature marriage of the burlesque with social commentary. Still debating with a silent adversary, the speaker suggests what lessons of history may lie in the most unassuming detail. And in doing so she asks us to reconsider what role we might directly play on the world stage. The speaker is questioning what it means to travel, what it means to "stay home and think of" the outside world; how "escapism" might reinforce or offer a corrective to an ethics of isolationism; how modern travel might contribute to, or make up for, the sins of colonial conquest.

The poem attempts to bring these subtle lessons to bear on what may appear to be the most indistinguishable local color because like all of Bishop's moralizing, the lessons are barely visible, hidden in dense landscapes and offhanded domestic dramas. She does not make explicit connections for us. Just as we are supplied with a vague theme—"democracy"—in her *Time-Life* text and left to momentarily ponder connections among "illegitimacy," "tolerance," "forbearance," and "trolley cars," so we are given "travel: pragmatics vs. aesthetics," then pieces of a social puzzle that we, like the speaker, are left to arrange as best we can. A similar buildup of mysteriously interrelated anecdotes and details characterizes the midsection of the poem; and just as Bishop directs us to contemplate the ethical and democratic implications of legitimizing the illegitimate in the *Brazil* text, the poem begins to draw us toward questions of history and natural responsibility.

The speaker has continued to hedge toward a contradiction where the "noble pantomimists" are concerned—"But surely it would have been a pity / not to have seen the trees along this road"—and the mild remonstrances in this excerpt rely on that first grammatic, as well as thematic, dissension to propel the empirical detail toward a final, mysterious sum of its parts.

> —Not to have had to stop for gas and heard
> the sad, two-noted, wooden tune
> of disparate wooden clogs
> carelessly clacking over
> a grease-stained filling-station floor.
> (In another country the clogs would all be tested.
> Each pair there would have identical pitch.)
> —A pity not to have heard
> the other, less primitive music of the fat brown bird
> who sings above the broken gasoline pump
> in a bamboo church of Jesuit baroque:
> three towers, five silver crosses.
> —Yes, a pity not to have pondered,
> blurr'dly and inconclusively,
> on what connection can exist for centuries
> between the crudest wooden footwear
> and, careful and finicky,
> the whittled fantasies of wooden cages. (94)

Still grappling with her split allegiances in the form of comparatives, the speaker's arguments seem to come increasingly from her heart rather than her head. The sudden sound of the "wooden clogs" with their "two-noted, wooden tune" is "sad," yet what could be sadder, the speaker seems to suggest in her aside, than a tuneless pair of "tested" ones with "identical pitch"? For a North American audience that tends to bank on its originality and prides itself on defying its ancestors—in this case perhaps the exacting Dutch—the choice would be clear.

The heart, that traditional site of the poetic impulse, is a deceptive organ. What moves it is as complex as anything that stimulates the mind. And in this case, as in all of Bishop's poetry, the two are inextricably tied. It is the "disparate" pitch of the clogs that paradoxically gives them their most alliterative poetic quality as they go "carelessly clacking over a grease-stained filling-station floor," stimulating the speaker's imagination with their uneven music. Yet like the modern historian or the ethnographer, who looks upon anomalies as doors, who seizes on data that disrupt rather than reiterate tradition, the traveler with the intense senses of the writer hears and then sees something rich in a place another tourist might avoid for sanitary reasons.[2] Although she registers the aesthetic peculiarities of the place, she also dwells on the potential historical ramifications of those same particulars.

VI

Wooden clogs appear in chapter eight of Bishop's *Time-Life Brazil* text in the context of a discussion on racial assimilation and the "colonial." And a brief foray into her discussion of them will lend historical resonance to what are finally not so casual observations. Twenty meticulous lines are dedicated to the material context and synaesthetic effect of this crude footwear. Thus we are urged beyond the idle amusements of cultural tourism toward a more complex understanding of the historical-political moment the speaker becomes witness to in her travels.

Bishop tells us that the "usual costume" of Portuguese men who pushed handcarts around the cities delivering freight—*burros sem rabos*, "donkeys without tails"—consisted of "wooden clogs, wide trousers, undershirts and large floppy berets" (*Brazil* 115). These Portuguese immigrants to Brazil, who in 1962 numbered 17,000 a year, made up a large part of the labor class. And this reference in the *Brazil* text offers one suggestion for "what connection can exist for centuries / between the crudest wooden footwear / and, careful and finicky, / the whittled fantasies of wooden cages," even if it is not conclusive. The connection hinges on the colonial occupation of Brazil, an occupation—like all occupations—both mercenary and holy in spirit.

In Bishop's poem "Brazil, January 1, 1502," we meet the ancestors of this gas station attendant—the first Portuguese Christian conquerors of Brazil. The new country, the speaker tells us, strikes the armored Christians, "hard as nails / tiny as nails," as "not unfamiliar"

but corresponding, nevertheless,
to an old dream of wealth and luxury
already out of style when they left home—
wealth, plus a brand-new pleasure. (*The Collected Poems* 92)

Expressly, the carrying off of Indian girls, a fact of colonial history Bishop also underscores in the *Brazil* text. Although Bishop has been accused of being insensitive to the plight of the poor in Brazil, this section of "Questions of Travel" contains densely layered historical references to the human condition in postcolonial Brazil. Part of the power of these twenty lines is not the accumulating mystery of the imagery but the very real and political narrative couched within. The poem brings us to the more recent phase of Brazil's struggle with its heritage: the poverty people are reduced to when the gold rush is over and the land is spent.

As elsewhere, the activities of Jesuit missionaries in Brazil paralleled geographically and chronologically those of these Portuguese colonizing powers in the sixteenth century. Between 1541 and 1556, Jesuit priests founded numerous missions under St. Ignatius throughout Brazil, where their primary business was to propagate the faith by instructing the unlettered on Christian principle. Thus "finicky" wooden cages of "Jesuit baroque" tell a haphazard story of the fate of the Catholic Church in colonial Brazil. Although the Church was more expensive adornment than benevolent social institution, Bishop does not necessarily dismiss the practical function of such useless beauty in the everyday existence of a struggling population. Like "the big dim doily" of "Filling Station" in the second part of the collection, the birdcage seems to offer evidence of a noble, although misguided but not altogether failed, principle at the heart of the spiritual impulse.

Yet from sixteenth-century Christian conqueror to twentieth-century pump jockey, the social record of the Portuguese in Brazil cannot be considered unequivocally progressive. And finally, the predatory nature of colonialism, which "civilizes" foreign lands for the higher purposes of church and state, eventually begins to gnaw on its own entrails. It is no accident, figurative or factual, that the wooden clogs clack over "a grease-stained filling-station floor" or that the birdcage hangs above "the broken gasoline pump." "Developing" countries like Brazil are the new colonies in the post–World War II economic order in which Ford and Mobil Oil are the latest victor-conquerors. Yet in such an order, modern necessities like cars and filling stations become isolated environmental disasters for those who cannot afford the upkeep, let alone keep up with their northern neighbors. The question of poverty confronts all North Americans who go south; it is something glimpsed through the window of a rented car.

In another instance in which crystalline prose and raw honesty converge in the *Time-Life* text, Bishop notes that North Americans often have difficulty assessing other nations' economic difficulties:

> It is hard, perhaps impossible, for rich nations to understand poor ones, and this is something that North Americans, with all their good intentions, often fail to realize. National poverty can produce the same symptoms and reactions everywhere—in Sicily or India, for example, as well as in Brazil. Anything a foreigner questions in Brazil—from inefficiency to dirt, from unpainted public buildings to rude bus drivers, from bad transportation to the water shortage—he is likely to blame on "the national character," or on the government's lack of concern for the people's welfare. But before he does so, he should ask himself, Can this be explained simply by poverty? Nine times out of ten it can. (*Brazil* 147)

Nowhere else do we find such a bold, unambiguous expression of Bishop's economic theory of social welfare. It is perhaps even more impossible for some North Americans to imagine that their clean living might depend on or result in the economic and social degradation of others. Yet far from projecting a nostalgia for the pastoral or preindustrial onto Brazil—another kind of colonial attitude toward subjected nations—Bishop argues that North Americans should question not only the supreme value of their national achievements but also the attendant arrogance that allows them to judge the "failures" of others. Again, what we notice about a country—"the dirt," "the water shortage"—may say more about our ignorance of International Monetary Fund policies than anything enlightening about the local color. Acknowledging that "industrialization is inevitable" in Brazil, Bishop nevertheless adds, "For now human-man is still more important than producing-man, or consuming-man or political-man" (*One Art* 400; *Brazil* 148). Thus what the onlooker does with the material conditions of a culture, the "grease-stained" floor, "the broken gasoline pump," will say everything about her breadth of historical and political understanding or her willingness to learn.

The information she is registering may not be available to the abstract philosopher or the armchair scholar. In a rare moment when Bishop actually defends the observational habits of women, she holds up the Baroque in contradistinction to other styles of representation:

> When it comes to a choice between a baroque chapel, and say Allen Tate—give me the chapel . . . while it's under our nose, I mean. But it is my chief complaint against the opposite sex, anyway—with the exception of poets and painters—they don't *see* things. They're always

having ideas & theories, and not noticing the detail at hand. . . . I have
a small theory of my own about this—that women have been *confined*,
mostly—and in confinement details count.—They *have* to see the
baby's ear; sewing *makes* you look closely.—They've had to do so much
appeasing they do feel moods quickly, etc. There may be nothing in it,
and as I said,—it doesn't apply to artists, or not good ones. (Harrison 227)

How we observe the world and, consequently, what we find there may depend
on the conditions of our own fostering; when we learn to look, we find.
Respecting the detail at hand, the observing traveler thus gleans information
in unorthodox ways, and what may appear fastidious and inconsequential to
the classical mind trained to filter observation through comprehensive ideas
may nevertheless prove theoretically compelling.

"A poet's mind is constantly amalgamating disparate experience," Eliot
suggests, and in the poem the speaker's mind is enthralled with all the
possible correspondences or paradoxes these disparate notes and collateral
articles promise. Her ears lead her to a visual discovery—the "fat brown
bird" that "sings" (an odd, timeless choice of verbs), in spite of, one would
think, "the broken gasoline pump" in that sudden, unearthly cage: "a bam-
boo church of Jesuit baroque." Although she can only begin to wonder
about the complex historical connections between these objects in the time
it takes to fill a rusty tank, she is more than happy to "ponder" "blurr'dly
and inconclusively" for the present, knowing there is everything to learn in
this humble, even doubtful foreign experience.

As if to reinforce the growing insistence on the value of direct, empirical experience, the language remains relatively accessible and prosaic. Like
the poem's opening stanza, however, there are momentary poetic excesses
that again add a special music to the speaker's lament. The cumbersome
present perfect grammar that the first lines repeat like a mantra and that
frames the memory as a whole ("to have seen," "to have seen," "to have had
to stop," "to have heard," "to have pondered") is smoothed out in the regular iambs of the car's arrival at the gas station, thus lending a resonating
aural appeal to the unpoetic mundanity of filling stations.

One characteristic of the present perfect tense, however, is that it in-
volves an indefinite span of time. Although an action may have begun in
the past—and in the case of the poem, the present perfect is necessary to
contrast with the simple past tense of each consecutive discovery—the action's
repercussions are still very much alive in the present. There is no final
simple past for them to vanish into. These filling stations, whether in Brazil or in the United States, are the sites of peculiar knowledge for each
speaker in each poem—knowledge that is enduring and vital to the present—

even if they may seem too crude to count as landmarks in the history of Western ideas.

One thing we might learn from the "connection that can exist for centuries" among funny shoes, whimsical architecture for pets, and modern petroleum fallout is that progress is a relative term. And in the poem the whole mess—and it is a mess—becomes a mosaic of the vestiges of colonialism that are as aesthetically arresting as they are politically cogent. It is not only in the activist press or official reports that we find evidence of the fact that petrol companies have made subjects of us all but also in the actual and everyday evidence of our dull, although complicated, lives. If this filling station, like the one up North, contains strange evidence that "someone loves us all," it is perhaps only in the loving eye of the beholder who listens and reads the rich lessons "in the weak calligraphy of songbirds' cages." Who else cares enough to study the grease stains and the chaos? How much is so easily and conveniently forgotten in the race for perfection?

As important as this cultural-historical context of the poem's stanza is the fact that history—the kind we conscript to textbooks or wait for experts to interpret—is often available in domestic remnants, fantastic artifacts, the disparate physical details that dovetail in the least probable places. And the central problem of the poem "Questions of Travel," the question "Should we have stayed at home and thought of here?" is partially answered. No, she is working herself up to say. Sometimes we must go look and listen, have immediate physical contact with the evidence of our best and worst theories—because not to do such fieldwork would be dishonest, and, finally, it *would* be a pity

—Never to have studied history in
the weak calligraphy of songbirds' cages. (94)

Acknowledging her student status—her questions, after all, have been a record of her studies—the speaker comes to the end of her worldly investigations. Her call for guidance has led her to trust increasingly in her earthly instincts.

Through her equivocation, she has been suggesting that reaching beyond the facts and reason of home when we are outside is a necessary, although difficult, enterprise. Trusting the disparate detail, even if only to "ponder" "blurr'dly and inconclusively" rather than decisively interpret the complexities of art and history, means focusing on the processes of history, allowing that connections—however accidental—can exist in the most unlikely discrepancies of time and place. Considering the world in terms usually limited to the aesthetic thus permits us to move beyond the limitations of traditional social scientific investigation.

VII

It is at this point that "the traveller takes a notebook" and records a new set of questions, ones that lend even more philosophical gravity to her previous questions of travel, aesthetics, history, and geopolitics. When the landscape takes leave of us in the form of a "sudden golden silence," the speaker fills it with a final answer to one adversary who has inhabited her conscience from the beginning and with whom she has been struggling to break free, or at least bridge a compromise. But now the voice is in quotations as if it were reported speech; it is italicized like a foreign language. There is a split in consciousness as the speaker confronts her own sense of homelessness.

> *"Is it lack of imagination that makes us come*
> *to imagined places, not just stay at home?*
> *Or could Pascal have been not entirely right*
> *about just sitting quietly in one's room?"* (97)

For one who questions her own motives, who fears her desire to seek abroad might really reflect the limp leitmotif that announces each remonstrance—merely "a pity" to do otherwise—these are difficult questions. If foreign travel is simply a "*divertissement*," as Pascal suggests in *Pensées*, an escape from the tragic sense of life by losing oneself in diversions, then yes, maybe it is a sign of lack of imagination. And to anybody suspicious of foreign travel as a colonial impulse to possess the exotic, particularly for domestic consumption, these are also heavy questions. Pascal, who did not approve of the Jesuits' penchant for travel, also notes that our restlessness, which is really the result of mankind's general anxiety and is behind our desire to escape, may also lead to political turmoil and war because "[a]ll the misery of man comes from this one thing—the inability to remain at peace in a room."

This is the voice that has been interrupting her pleasure in the physical beauty of Brazil and the intellectual attraction of its cultural vagaries. And this higher rationalization, the source of her guilt, does give her reason enough to hesitate. Within this divided consciousness, however, comes a sudden formal response in language. In the almost perfect aaba ccac rhyme scheme (come, home, right, room; society, free, home, be), the speaker suddenly imposes rather strict rhetorical limitations on her counterargument. A more formal prosody now becomes the site of tension in a wonderful final reversal of language roles.

Where poetic excesses had signaled moments of impulsive resistance earlier in the poem, this sudden Formalist conclusion now strikes us as oddly traditional, as if the speaker were capitulating to rational demands beyond the poem's own inconclusive logic. But because the poem's anecdotal, digressive reasoning has not unfolded in formal terms until now, we suspect this sudden regular rhyme scheme is another attempt at resistance. Perhaps such linguistic order may appeal to that other voice, may speak to it in cadences that satisfy its need to control the chaos that has permeated its borders. Yet even if the speaker is responding in language that would appeal to a traditional audience, it is a divided voice. Just when we think we have located the poem's first pentameter couplet, the speaker twice throws in an informal "just," spoiling any rage for order we might harbor. The effect is something akin to the mastery, careful but strained, of a foreign tongue. The speaker may suddenly observe certain rules of discourse, but she will continue to undermine the isolationist theories that have kept her voice in check.

Pascal also argued that history was directed more by the insignificant trifle or chance accident than people wished to believe. Just as a "grain of sand" in Cromwell's organs rather than a particular decree or planned advance changed European and Christian history, so might an overbooked boat or an allergic reaction to the cashew nut forever alter an individual's history. But if human history is really a question of the accidental, therefore irrational, rather than the logical, thus predictable, Pascal's answers to the questions of travel, his suggestion that we sit quietly in our rooms and think of here, are perhaps "not entirely right." In fact, there is a contradiction here that the speaker lights on and exploits for her own purposes.

The speaker's hesitation has been inscribed in part of the poem's grammar as a struggle between the experiential present and the conditional past perfect, an idealized state that assumes a stable point of reference. Finally, she must insist that home—like Pascal's notion of history—is an unstable concept, highly questionable physically and theoretically.

> Continent, city, country, society:
> the choice is never wide and never free.
> And here, or there . . . No. Should we have stayed at home,
> wherever that may be?" (94)

Without reference to that teleological seat of truth we call home, the speaker has had no choice but to commit herself to her immediate surroundings. She has had no choice but to *be* in uncertainties, doubts, and mysteries. Homelessness, even other than the kind that results from economic hardship, still inspires uneasiness; many read only anxiety and loss in the interstices of the word.

Yet homelessness, as Bishop shows us, may also open opportunities for new knowledge. When we are able to let go of the security of home, particularly its narratives of the outside world, we move from isolationism to internationalism. Accepting centerlessness as the natural state of things thus becomes not only one answer to the accidents of history but also perhaps the best imaginative response we can hope to muster to these questions of travel. The speaker has slyly shown us the lessons we learn when we know to stop and indulge ourselves in the aesthetics of petrol stations. Being in a country not your own extends you, Alastair Reid remembers Bishop saying: "It makes you look with far greater attention, far greater scrutiny. You have to notice things" (Reid in Fountain and Brazeau 182). The lessons, of course, are worldly, and Pascal in his later, ascetic years—when he wrote *Pensées*— was more interested in the afterlife. Yet his "theory of the imperceptible cause," his view that morality and truth are ultimately affected by accidents of geography and climate, offers the speaker an important relativistic an-swer to her questions of travel and, perhaps more important, her questions of asylum. If she has resisted that internalized voice of reason that says she should grow up and go home, she has shown us that it is through no choice of her own. Her stylistic and semantic hesitation has reflected that "quality" Keats suggests goes to form "A Man of Achievement": with no choice but to empathize with her immediate environment, the speaker, in the form of the poem, makes a virtue of necessity.

5
"Crusoe in England"

"THE LONG STORY
THAT NEVER COMES TO AN END"

A small boy alone under the mango trees,
I read the story of Robinson Crusoe.

—Carlos Drummond de Andrade

I

Daniel Defoe—Puritan pamphleteer, Tory spy—created a new literary form and reading public when he published *Robinson Crusoe* in 1719. In *Mapping Men and Empire*, Richard Phillips tells us that although it is perhaps one of the most influential adventure stories ever written in English, the book nevertheless made its biggest impression on geographical imaginations in the nineteenth century (23). A burst of "Robinsonades," or Robinson narratives, occurred in the Victorian period as *Robinson Crusoe* came to be read increasingly as a "metaphorical map of Britain" for the nineteenth century (31). Starting out a man with little identity, Crusoe is constructed on the island; and his ingenious dominion over his new, foreign environment becomes as integral to his "salvation" as his recognition of God's divine providence.

Phillips argues that Crusoe is not an invented identity but rather a "recasting and reasserting" of existent ones—"He leaves society, but society doesn't leave him" (31)—and this includes the presumptions and prejudices endemic to the missionary-mercenary spirit. Although Crusoe's shipwreck

83

occurs when he is on his way to the west coast of Africa to buy slaves for his plantation in Brazil, his later penitence will be in the name of patience and trust in God's will rather than for sins against humanity:

> What business had I to leave a settled fortune, a well-stocked planta-tion, improving and increasing, to turn supercargo to Guinea, to fetch Negroes, when patience and time would have brought them at our own door from those whose business it was to fetch them? And though it had cost us something more, yet the difference of that price was by no means worth saving at so great a hazard. (Defoe 174)

There is no ironic distance between speaker and Puritan author during this and many like moments of Eurocentric bigotry in the text. Racial superior-ity and economic dependency on slavery are unexamined, colonial givens.

When Crusoe does experience feelings of affection for "his man" Friday, he looks to scripture for an explanation and justification of the master-slave relationship he sometimes questions:

> For never man has [had] a more faithful, loving, sincere servant than Friday was to me; without passions, sullenness, or designs, perfectly obliged and engaged. . . . This frequently gave me occasion to observe, and that with wonder, that however it had pleased God, in His provi-dence, and in the government of His works of His hands, to take from so great a part of the world of His creatures the best uses to which their faculties and the powers of their souls are adapted, yet that He has bestowed upon them the same powers, the same reason, the same affections, the same sentiments of kindness and obligation . . . that He has given to us; and that when He please to offer to them occasions of exerting these, they are as ready, nay, more ready to apply them to the right uses for which they were bestowed than we are. And this made me very melancholy sometimes. . . . But I shut it up and checked my thoughts with this conclusion; first that we do not know by what light and law these should be condemned. (187)

In spite of this mild remonstrance—perhaps no small thing for a Puri-tan pamphleteer—the association of spiritual enlightenment with Brit-ish rule proves to be a priori knowledge for the reconstructed Crusoe, not wisdom he acquires later through trial and error. Sinning against his biological father (who had told him to stay home and dream of there) will become a typological figure for sinning against the penultimate fa-ther England in the text and, in turn, against God the Father. Yet although he offends against all three in straying from the British Isles, his tribula-tions advocate an isolationist international policy rather than a critique of colonialism.

Asked in a 1977 interview what had prompted her to write "Crusoe in England," Bishop replied:

> I don't know. I reread the book and discovered how really awful *Robinson Crusoe* was, which I hadn't realized. . . . I reread it all in one night. And I had forgotten it was so moral. All that Christianity. So I think I wanted to re-see it with all that left out. (Schwartz and Estess 319)

"Re-seeing" *Robinson Crusoe* will mean not simply leaving out Christian morality but subverting it and the other agents of reform that accompany or precede the evangelical impulse. As the poem rewrites the experience— physical, psychological, and emotional—of one of the most famous adventurer-explorers in English literature, it also confronts or challenges the culture that created him. The political problem motivating much of the poem's rhetoric is colonial ambition.

While the tone of the poem never strays far beyond the speaker's own anguish, Bishop borrows from the techniques of comedy to subvert the intertext and tell her Crusoe's story. This reimaging appeals to Aristophanes, Longinus, and Pope, but with a twist we often associate with Chekhov's dramatic characters or the Theater of the Absurd. Again and again she creates a bathetic rhetorical effect, a sudden unexpected sinking or flattening of sound and sense that undermines any more elevated conclusions a stanza might promise. And through structural innovation in the form of anticlimax, Bishop mocks the colonial enterprise.

The impulse behind the anticlimax as a rhetorical strategy is not a conservative one in Bishop's method. Rather than mock a subject or subjects who strive for a grandiloquence beyond their intellectual or ethical means, she employs anticlimax as a check on what mythological power Crusoe as a cultural hero might still hold over his audience. The result is an edgy, off-center poem that ultimately refuses to take its personal suffering, let alone any notion of divine vengeance, too seriously. And in encouraging the reader to do likewise, it suggests that we keep an arched brow turned to our own geographical imaginings, personal as well as political.

The poem begins in the beginning with the birth of an island that announces itself as "a mist from the earth" (*King James* 2.6):

> A new volcano has erupted,
> the papers say, and last week I was reading
> where some ship saw an island being born:
> at first a breath of steam, ten miles away;
> and then a black fleck—basalt, probably—
> rose in the mate's binoculars

and caught on the horizon like a fly.
They named it. But my poor old island's still
un-rediscovered, un-renamable.
None of the books has ever got it right. ("Crusoe in England," *The*
Collected Poems 162)

This subtle genesis is immediately pulled to earth by the exacting vocabulary of the naturalist who identifies the physical properties of the "black
fleck" before moving on to other, larger questions of naming and origins. As
the distant island rises in the mate's binoculars and then, as if transformed
into a sudden surreal tableau, "catches" on the horizon like a "fly," the
speaker abruptly replaces natural science with homely metaphorical allusion. The aesthetic distancing that preludes the bold, blunt act of classifica-
tion—"They named it"—is then self-consciously rejected in the stanza's
moody final line: "None of the books has ever got it right." This first series
of bathetic statements parodies the complex drama of capturing a thing in a
name. In "setting the record straight" the speaker must run a gamut of
absurdly compiled pre-fixed and suf-fixed rhetorical states to locate the roots
of her experience. And like the three-beat line that will continue to jog
between hypermetrics and catalexis throughout the poem, the reimagining
of the Defoe text will lurch between tragic participation in the ideals pur-
sued in the intertext and a comic distancing from those ideals that perceives
the incongruities in the colonial narratives that "cover" and "name" the
island adventure.

Bishop was serious about anticlimactic endings in poetry and was not
humorless about the poem's power to signify in traditional ways. The poet
Sandra McPherson, who studied with Bishop at the University of Washing-
ton, comments on Bishop's playful "irreverence": "I have a sense that the
voice in her own poetry is amused, and that she was secretly laughing to
herself, enjoying things" (McPherson in Fountain and Brazeau 211). Read
against the Puritan earnestness of Defoe's hero, Bishop's Crusoe is a grin-
ning heretic, and never more so than when he refuses to rise to the climactic occasion of his insights. McPherson discusses Bishop's theory on last
lines, one structural explanation for the wry play we sense in Crusoe's voice:

Elizabeth said, "Why always save your best line for last? Put it second to
last." She encouraged me to see that the drama of a poem can have a
little different shape than I had thought. It doesn't always have to build
up to that high point. If you're writing really well, you have high points
all the way through the poem. In her work, every place in the poem
gives pleasure. It doesn't have to build up to some huge insight.
(McPherson in Fountain and Brazeau 211–212)

Even if Bishop's writing does not strike us with its sexual-textual aban-
don—a libidinal Feminist writing McPherson perhaps inadvertently suggests—this conception of poetic drama, and this poem's playing out of it in
particular, nonetheless suggest that the refusal to adopt those traditional
literary structures that inscribe such classics as the *Robinson Crusoe* intertext
also signals a search for alternative visions of cultural freedom. A conscious
avoidance of "building up to huge insights"—the kind that concludes most
chapters in the Defoe text—leaves Bishop's poem free to explore the under-
side of these same convictions. Multiclimax (often folded within the deceptive hush of parentheses in her poems), punctuated by anticlimax, winks at
her antihero's dilemmas, allowing the speaker to engage in the moral consequences of cultural estrangement while resisting Defoe's hegemonic response
to otherness.

The next stanza of the poem offers fine examples of multiple high points
of textual pleasure—pleasure, as is often the case in Bishop's poems, that
registers in close proximity with the profane.

> Well, I had fifty-two
> miserable, small volcanoes I could climb
> with a few slithery strides—
> volcanoes dead as ash heaps.
> I used to sit on the edge of the highest one
> and count the others standing up,
> naked and leaden, with their heads blown off.
> I'd think that if they were the size
> I thought volcanoes should be, then I had
> become a giant;
> and if I had become a giant,
> I couldn't bear to think what size
> the goats and turtles were,
> or the gulls, or the overlapping rollers
> —a glittering hexagon of rollers
> closing and closing in, but never quite,
> glittering and glittering, though the sky
> was mostly overcast. (*The Collected Poems* 162)

The sudden brutality of the seventh line has the final effect of a last blast,
the kind Max Beerbohm in his 1900 essay on anticlimax, "Last Acts," says
audiences prefer because it allows them to "leave the theatre as excitedly as
though [they] were being shot from the mouth of a cannon" (101). But in
reducing the line's dramatic potential by placing it midstanza, Bishop allows
violence to inhabit—as if quite naturally—the very interstices of the textual landscape. It is grammatically unclear if it is the "I" that is "naked and

leaden" or the small volcanoes; thus the black-humored potential of things standing up "with their heads blown off" is twofold, pointing simultaneously, as it does, to the speaker's mental condition. Like Dickinson's "Hour of lead— / Remembered, if outlived," there is a quarrel with memory in these lines. Crusoe's present lethargy, his final "hour of lead," as we will see, puts his earlier emotional trauma into hyper-real perspective. It will prove preferable to the real despondency he experiences in safety. Like Dickinson, Bishop will sometimes turn to violence for the temporary resolve it affords survivors.

In contrast to this first climax, the buildup that follows dissolves into an offhand comment about the weather. There is no attempt to resolve the growing hysteria that accompanies the Kafkaesque shift in scale. David Kalstone notes that Bishop's shifts in perspective and "confusion of properties" point to the fragility and provisional nature of human observation. In this case, however, the speaker seems to parody Bishop's own discursive habits by making a hallucinatory mockery of proportion. Like the Man-Moth who lacks aesthetic distance from his surreal environment, which in turn threatens to consume him,

> He thinks the moon is a small hole at the top of the sky,
> proving the sky quite useless for protection. ("The Man-Moth*," *The Collected Poems* 14)

Crusoe is haunted by the early memories of lost perspective on the island. But as Kalstone also argues, instead of unsettling our perspective as readers, Bishop's shifts tend to strengthen our understanding of whatever problem she has set out to explore. The semiotic complexities begin to divulge themselves at the moment when mimesis breaks down, and as Crusoe metamorphoses from the synecdochic political subject in Defoe's text to the less immediately qualifiable human subject in Bishop's text, the narrative becomes increasingly irreverent and riotous. These shifts in scale reveal the subject's inability to impose rational models of thought on his environment. Yet this lack of control strikes us as a form of liberation from the kind of fear-induced aggressiveness toward the landscape we see in Defoe's tale. This speaker's fear, like Alice's fear in Wonderland, tends to be quickly displaced by amazement at or admiration for the strange beauty found in unusual proportions. And any dreams of grandeur the speaker may be tempted to entertain are put into perspective, as it were, by rival animate forms— giant goats and gulls.

In the next stanza Bishop offers various examples of national, domestic iconography that recirculate the "breath of steam" as figurative life source in the poem's cultural landscape. They also become objects of derision.

My island seemed to be
a sort of cloud-dump. All the hemisphere's
left-over clouds arrived and hung
above the craters—their parched throats
were hot to touch.
Was that why it rained so much?
And why sometimes the whole place hissed?
The turtles lumbered by, high-domed,
hissing like teakettles.
(And I'd have given years, or taken a few,
for any sort of kettle, of course.)
The folds of lava, running out to sea,
would hiss. I'd turn. And then they'd prove
to be more turtles.
The beaches were all lava, variegated,
black, red, and white, and gray;
the marbled colors made a fine display. ("Crusoe in England," *The
Collected Poems* 162–163)

The repressed wish behind the first dreamlike vision of the hissing turtles
(and there will be more) reveals itself in the ubiquitous British teakettle.
Unlike Defoe's Crusoe, who devotes much of his tale to the description of
his rudimentary crafting of domestic items, Bishop's Crusoe directly confesses the passionate extent of his longing to re-create a British heaven on
the all-too-earthly island.

As if to satirize his yearning for his own native rituals, which the teakettle as sign projects onto the poem, the speaker—in the form of a sudden,
unprecedented, perfectly rhymed couplet—impetuously imposes the type of
comparatives one might find in *Ladies Home Journal* where fabricated nature
is often preferred for its aesthetic appeal without the mess: "black, red, and
white, and gray; / the marbled colors made a fine display." The isolated
preciosity among lumbering sea turtles and molten lava strikes us as out of
place, if not playfully ridiculous.

Later, when the speaker pauses for a bit of wanton navel gazing, his
imperfect attempts to put this longing for home into existential perspective
are abandoned for a similar kind of forced, neurotic closure, reinforced by a
similar kind of final—although less-than-perfect—rhyme.

I often gave way to self-pity.
"Do I deserve this? I suppose I must.
I wouldn't be here otherwise. Was there
a moment when I actually chose this?
I don't remember, but there could have been."

What's wrong about self-pity, anyway?
With my legs dangling down familiarly
over a crater's edge, I told myself
"Pity should begin at home." So the more
pity I felt, the more I felt at home. (163)

Like a surrealist debate on necessity and choice, language is reduced to such
a scale that two of humankind's most fundamental questions appear unin-
spired, if not pathetic. Gone are the profound nouns and ponderous verbs
usually dedicated to such meditations. There is no movement toward rational conclusion or completion that would imply an orderly world of cause
and effect, of beginnings and endings. If one impulse behind the rhetorical
reductiveness of, say, Beckett's dialogues is an overwhelming sense of the
loneliness and impotence modern man must face without God or the opti-
mistic rationalism necessary to pluck his courage, then Crusoe's absurdist
character is striking in this stanza. Action, mental and physical, folds on
itself, refusing to aspire to more than unanswered questions on the crater's
edge.

And one can almost hear the snare drum punctuate the pun on home-
spun Christian wisdom, "Charity should begin at home." The slapstick response converts the stanza's tragic potential into a comic reading of itself.
These musings on existential isolation are not given the benefit of tragic
doubt in the existence of fate or free will. Rather, the comic perception of
incongruity riotously undermines whatever embattled idealism the speaker
may still harbor. The philosophical pun that concludes this stanza is reinforced in the mock syllogistic logic of its rhetoric: "'Pity should begin at
home.' So the more / pity I felt, the more I felt at home." Unlike Defoe's
Crusoe, who profits from his isolation by combating and overcoming self-
pity through the acceptance of God or Nature's greater design, Bishop's
Crusoe makes a secular joke out of his own shortcomings by parodying his
egocentrism. Rather than surmount his difficulties through a typological
interpretation of them, he chooses to wallow in self-knowledge.

This playful, absurdist remedy to the problem of isolation carries on
into the tautological nursery rhyme that introduces the next stanza.

The sun set in the sea; the same odd sun
rose from the sea,
and there was one of it and one of me.
The island had one kind of everything:
one tree snail, a bright violet-blue
with a thin shell, crept over everything,
over the one variety of tree,

a sooty, scrub affair.
Snail shells lay under these in drifts
and, at a distance,
you'd swear that they were beds of irises. (163–164)

Reducing experience to a Lewis Carroll–like romp with solitude as a figure, Bishop's Crusoe makes an absurdist joke out of the number one. Yet when he gives in to "depravity" to assuage his loneliness, something Defoe never allows his Protestant hero to do, his home-brew–inspired bacchanalia gathers together various recurring threads in the intertext and gives them a pluralistic, pagan spin.

There was one kind of berry, a dark red.
I tried it, one by one, and hours apart.
Sub-acid, and not bad, no ill effects;
and so I made home-brew. I'd drink
the awful, fizzy, stinging stuff
that went straight to my head
and play my home-made flute
(I think it had the weirdest scale on earth)
and, dizzy, whoop and dance among the goats.
Home-made, home-made! But aren't we all?
I felt a deep affection for
the smallest of my island industries.
No, not exactly, since the smallest was
a miserable philosophy. (164)

The goats, moonshine, and "savages" who "whoop and dance" and appear and disappear in the intertext like so many covert subtexts come together here under one urge. Adopting the "barbarous gestures" of those whom Defoe's Crusoe, in his right mind, would enslave, Bishop's Crusoe—like a follower of Dionysius, the "outsider" god—momentarily loses himself in a vision of ecstatic universalism: "Home-made, home-made! But aren't we all?" (Defoe 180). When he is sober, however, the memory palls and the lonely "I" returns, attempting to right itself with a bit of utilitarian conviction—something to atone for the momentary carnal lapse. But once again the stanza drifts off as if unsatisfied with its own false compromises.

This Crusoe is, in fact, overwhelmed and tortured by his natural environment. The potentially bucolic island with its goats and gulls and turtles becomes for him a synaesthetic nightmare:

The island smelled of goat and guano.
The goats were white, so were the gulls,
and both too tame, or else they thought

I was a goat, too, or a gull.
Baa, baa, baa and shriek, shriek, shriek,
baa . . . shriek . . . baa . . . I still can't shake
them from my ears; they're hurting now.
The questioning shrieks, the equivocal replies
over a ground of hissing rain
and hissing, ambulating turtles
got on my nerves. (164)

There is hysteria in the repetitive consonants and redundant, inverted vocabulary. And just when the speaker's nerves seem to be going the way of
the turtles, he lapses into yet one more nostalgic reverie of England:

When all the gulls flew up at once, they sounded
like a big tree in a strong wind, its leaves.
I'd shut my eyes and think about a tree,
an oak, say, with real shade, somewhere.
I'd heard of cattle getting island-sick.
I thought the goats were.
One billy-goat would stand on the volcano
I'd christened Mont d'Espoir or Mount Despair
(I'd time enough to play with names),
and bleat and bleat, and sniff the air.
I'd grab his beard and look at him.
His pupils, horizontal, narrowed up
and expressed nothing, or a little malice. (165)

The christening process becomes a game of mistranslation, "hope" in French,
"despair" in English. And the goat as Teiresias, or wise man, whom suppli-
cants approached with a tug on the beard, is yet another unsuccessful attempt to impress familiar narratives on the immediate, bleak surface of the
landscape.

Crusoe's inability to successfully manipulate his environment through
acts of aesthetic sabotage—

I got so tired of the very colors!
One day I dyed a baby goat bright red
with my red berries, just to see
something a little different.
And then his mother wouldn't recognize him. (165)

—brings on other nightmares of death, birth, and the registration of them.

Dreams were the worst. Of course I dreamed of food
and love, but they were pleasant rather

than otherwise. But then I'd dream of things
like slitting a baby's throat, mistaking it
for a baby goat. . . . (165)

In this slanted inversion of the biblical story in which God substitutes a
ram for the sacrificial son, Bishop shocks us with yet another brutal image
of decapitation. Feeling a victim of his environment, the speaker paradoxically turns out to be the executioner, his wish fulfillment semiotically reinforced with a linguistic slippage between the rhyming phrases "baby's throat"
and "baby goat." Out of his own mind, he imagines a world in which bodies
and heads are separated entities as a result of enormous miscalculations.

In the Defoe intertext the hero spends much time ruminating on the
evils of human sacrifice: "The place was covered with human bones, the
ground dyed with their blood" (186). Yet although Friday is allowed to explain the ritual of postwar sacrifice and cannibalism in the Caribees—"They
no eat mans but when make the war fight" (200)—the hero cannot recon-
cile this information with another form of national violence, that practiced
by the Spaniards in the Americas:

> [T]hey destroyed millions of these people, who, however they were
> idolaters and barbarians and had several bloody and barbarous rites in
> their customs, such as sacrificing human bodies to their idols, were yet,
> as to the Spaniards, very innocent people. (154)

When others eventually arrive on his island and Crusoe establishes his own
kingdom, he will nonetheless place a Spaniard over the "idolaters and bar-
barians" in his symbolic chain of command. While Bishop's Crusoe has
similar blood on his hands in his dream of sacrifice, in confusing his victims
Bishop's speaker makes a mockery of premeditated violence, what Defoe's
hero distinctly sets apart and condones as "National punishments" (155).
Violent sacrificial death, with its distant echo of territory wars and national
disputes in the intertext, leads to an obsessive dream of geographical over-
abundance.

> . . . I'd have
> nightmares of other islands
> stretching away from mine, infinities
> of islands, islands spawning islands,
> like frogs' eggs turning into polliwogs
> of islands, knowing that I had to live
> on each and every one, eventually,
> for ages, registering their flora,
> their fauna, their geography. (165)

A nightmarish female fertility overcompensates for what is always lack-ing in a dream of empire: earth. Yet we cannot help but see Darwin raising his distracted head here. As the quintessential registrar of flora and fauna, Darwin is also a writer Bishop admired, if only for his discursive style:

> [R]eading Darwin one admires the beautiful solid case being built up out of his endless, heroic observations, almost unconscious or auto-matic—and then comes a sudden relaxation, a forgetful phrase, and one feels that strangeness of his undertaking, sees the lonely young man, his eye fixed on facts and minute details, sinking or sliding giddily off into the unknown. (Bishop in Kalstone, *Becoming a Poet* 15)

This "sinking or sliding" also describes Bishop's own formal arrangement of the poem. And what is disturbing in this stanza's fitful language is the hyperconscious attention to detail that goes unrelieved by the bathetic state-ment that until now has characterized her endings. Images of violence and furious reproduction, death and birth, remain locked in a relentless cycle in this section.

Yet even here there is a certain trace of mockery, this time self-directed if we consider these lines from a hypertextual point of view. Emulating Darwin and his delicate eye in her own careful aesthetic, Bishop also wor-ried that her descriptions could begin to resemble the less interesting side of Darwin's prose, the endless cataloging that is the business of the naturalist. This self-parody adds flavor to a nightmare of banishment and chronicling. Like Darwin, Bishop was a recorder of geography; and like Darwin, her life would become intricately entwined in the history and politics of other cul-tures. Social Darwinism would offer pseudoscientific justification for the continued oppression of peoples worldwide. And the poet, like the scien-tist, finds herself embroiled in questions of national interest, regardless of any overt claims of disinterestedness or objectivity. The flip side of the dream of discovery is the nightmare of conscience. Geographical mapping, instigated by human sacrifice, becomes the inherited bane of the recorder-poet.

II

Friday's arrival in the poem has a distinct calming effect on what has be-come an increasingly angst-ridden rhetoric. Like an angel of mercy he helps relieve Crusoe of his biggest burden—himself—by forcing him to divide his attention in two.

> ... when I thought I couldn't stand it
> another minute longer, Friday came.

(Accounts of that have everything all wrong.)
Friday was nice.
Friday was nice, and we were friends.
If only he had been a woman!
I wanted to propagate my kind,
and so did he, I think, poor boy.
He'd pet the baby goats sometimes,
and race with them, or carry one around.
—Pretty to watch; he had a pretty body. (165–166)

Critics tend to focus on the autobiographical signification of the child imagery in this part of the poem.[1] And there are homoerotic undercurrents in Crusoe's response to Friday.[2] Perhaps equally interesting in the homoeroticism of the stanza is how dramatically it "re-sees" the traditional narrative, particularly the way in which the latter introduces Friday:

> He was a comely, handsome fellow, perfectly well made, with straight strong limbs, not too large; tall and well-shaped, and, as I reckon, about twenty-six years of age. He had a good countenance, not a fierce and surly aspect; but seemed to have something very manly in his face, and yet he had all the sweetness and softness of an European in his countenance too, especially when he smiled. His hair was long and black, not curled like wool; his forehead very high and large; and a great vivacity and sparkling sharpness in his eyes. The color of his skin was not quite black, but very tawny; and yet not an ugly, yellow, nauseous tawny, as the Brazilians and Virginians, and other natives of America are. . . . His face was round and plump; his nose small, not flat like the Negroes: a very good mouth, thin lips, and his fine teeth well set, and white as ivory. (Defoe 184)

An unsettling combination of desire and racism, this construction of a perfect "other"—one who is enough like Anglo-Europeans (not too black) to merit admiration yet different enough to relegate him to servitude—bears within it the seeds of the simple assessment of Friday in Bishop's poem—"Pretty to watch; he had a pretty body." Bishop's Crusoe, however, rejects the master-servant relationship—"(Accounts of that have everything all wrong.)"—and instead creates for a brief moment an image of domestic bliss that is ultimately the poem's gravitational center. This is the stanza from which every other stanza in the poem falls away. For a brief moment the discrepancy that has existed until now between the speaker's intentions (the re-creation, for example, of an English island) and the speaker's actions or inaction (mental and physical) suddenly dissolves, leaving him socially engaged, delightfully unself-conscious about his human desires: "I wanted

to propagate my kind, / and so did he, I think, poor boy." Bathos is suspended for as long as lover and beloved are left to exist simply in nature
beyond the reaches of church and state.

> And then one day they came and took us off. (166)

When this tragic moment comes—the return to solitude dramatized in
the line's spatial offsetting—the understated loss is painfully effective. The
rest is denouement. The comedy ends as a dirgelike solemnity takes us back
to England and Crusoe's life without Friday.

> Now I live here, another island,
> that doesn't seem like one, but who decides?
> My blood was full of them; my brain
> bred islands. But that archipelago
> has petered out. I'm old.
> I'm bored, too, drinking my real tea,
> surrounded by uninteresting lumber.
> The knife there on the shelf—
> it reeked of meaning, like a crucifix.
> It lived. How many times did I
> beg it, implore it, not to break?
> I knew each nick and scratch by heart,
> the bluish blade, the broken tip,
> the lines of wood-grain on the handle . . .
> Now it won't look at me at all.
> The living soul has dribbled away.
> My eyes rest on it and pass on. (166)

Lines after Friday are less ironic than lines before Friday. Native products
and rituals lack the kind of aesthetic distance that made desire and humor
possible. They are simply there, in dreary succession. Things he pined after,
such as "real tea" (no more hissing teapot turtles), lapse into habits that no
longer comfort or satisfy his taste for the "exotic." Things Crusoe once
hated, the burgeoning "archipelago," are now dear because of their association with a time and place that animated even lifeless objects with more
than a functional reason to be. If Defoe's hero experiences a spiritual awakening on the island, so does Bishop's antihero. Awakening to the redemp-
tive potential of human love, Bishop's Crusoe moves beyond the prejudices
endemic to Christian morality and couples with a pagan. Objects like the
knife that are synecdoches for the brute hardships of physical isolation rise
to the signifying power of religious relics in the wake of emotional conquest.
But taken out of their working contexts, which prove to be spiritual as well

as physical complexes—"Now it won't look at me at all. / The living soul
has dribbled away"—objects, like people, die.

Robinson Crusoe may continue to circulate in the narratives of Christian Europeans, but he is, after all—like the knife—an iconographic item of
colonial history, a dead relic.

> The local museum's asked me to
> leave everything to them:
> the flute, the knife, the shrivelled shoes,
> my shedding goatskin trousers
> (moths have got in the fur),
> the parasol that took me such a time
> remembering the way the ribs should go.
> It still will work but, folded up,
> looks like a plucked and skinny fowl.
> How can anyone want such things? (166)

Other objects central to the intertext, particularly the parasol, are, like
Crusoe, interesting remnants from another age but inert in their present
postcolonial condition. Historical paraphernalia are only as useful as readers are competent to interpret them. And in the case of this Crusoe, our
knowledge of the revised version of his "adventure" endows these articles
with the potential to signify beyond the limited narratives of "reconstructed"
Christian colonists. Because in "Crusoe in England" Bishop gives us a
deconstructed revision of an old tale, a "re-seeing" that will not allow vestiges of the colonial urge to sneak by without a solid dose of sardonic derision, we are urged to critically reevaluate the ascendancy of the intertext in
English letters. It is easy to forget "how really awful" much of it is but even
easier to forget the geopolitical circumstances that inscribe such narratives.
Although the poem offers no inquisitorial suggestion that we burn the original *Robinson Crusoe* or even take it off our shelves, it shows us how to laugh
at its arrogant assumptions and deadly rites.

"Crusoe in England" is, finally, tragicomical in the dramatic sense of the
term because, as John Fletcher defined it, it lacks death (the speaker as
antihero has survived to tell his tired, first-person tale) yet brings us close
enough to it, or an emotional semblance of it, "to make it no comedy."
Stripping away the heroic rhetoric of the inveterate conquistador, Bishop
reimagines the troubled spirit of the reimmigrant castaway. And the result-
ing tale is one of mishap and regret—one, however, that leads to a more
genuine knowledge of the small self that inhabits the imperial clothing than
we see in the classic text. But to humanize the hero, Bishop has had to pull
the proverbial carpet out from underneath the culture that created Crusoe.

III

Included in Bishop's *Collected Poems* is a translation from the Portuguese of a poem by Carlos Drummond de Andrade entitled "Infancy." We find here another re-seeing of *Robinson Crusoe* that speaks of the complexities of colonialism and race. Written by a mulatto Brazilian poet, the poem reflects on the mixed ancestry of his country's population and the hierarchical social systems that still dictate relations between people after 400 years.

My father got on his horse and went to the field.
My mother stayed sitting and sewing.
My little brother slept.
A small boy alone under the mango trees,
I read the story of Robinson Crusoe,
the long story that never comes to an end.

At noon, white with light, a voice that had learned
lullabies long ago in the slave-quarters—and never forgot—
called us for coffee.
Coffee blacker than the black old woman
delicious coffee
good coffee.

My mother stayed sitting and sewing
watching me:
Shh—don't wake the boy.
She stopped the cradle when a mosquito had lit
and gave a sigh . . . how deep!
Away off there my father went riding
through the farm's endless wastes.

And I didn't know that my story
was prettier than that of Robinson Crusoe. (258)

And such may have been the offspring of Crusoe and Friday, a thoughtful little boy already creating aesthetic distance between himself and his parents. Quietly confronting the cultural narratives that inform the classic tale of adventure, isolation, and landed wealth, Andrade's child registers the interaction of black and white in his immediate environment. If his tale is "prettier," it is maybe because he, as the narrator, will one day be able to retell the story from the position of a less stable, thus more empathetic, subject; part insider, part outsider, he may approach his retelling from the position of subject as agent (Bhabha 185).

If malaria, the mosquito-borne disease so deadly to Europeans, threatens the baby in the poem, another disease brought from Europe to the

Americas and mortal to the indigenous population is what paradoxically dooms Crusoe's happiness:

—And Friday, my dear Friday, died of measles
seventeen years ago come March. (166)

And so ends the long poem about the riches and ravages of colonial conquest, "the long story that never comes to an end." In the course of the poem Crusoe has deflated his achievement and reputation as an enterprising explorer and merchant, and, more important, he has allowed us to read his story against that of the original. The bathetic revision of the heroic tale has allowed us to laugh at the absurdity of the colonial enterprise while keeping in mind that death, although momentarily transcended, may be only an island away.

Conclusion

Doubts of all things earthly, and intuitions of some things heavenly;
this combination makes neither believer nor infidel, but makes a man
who regards them both with equal eye.

—MELVILLE

I

BISHOP SHARES HER CRUSOE'S LACK OF FAITH IN IDEAS that aim to organize material culture too neatly. And both have much in common with that other itinerant writer, Herman Melville—not the least in his wry flair for laughing from time to time at his own intellectual pretensions. He says of the whale spout—Crusoe's "Glass Chimneys, flexible, attenuated, / sacerdotal beings of glass":

> He [the Sperm Whale] is both ponderous and profound. And I am
> convinced that from the heads of all ponderous profound beings, such
> as Plato, Pyrrho, the Devil, Jupiter, Dante, and so on, there always goes
> up a certain semi-visible steam, while in the act of thinking deep
> thoughts. While in the act of composing a little treatise on Eternity, I
> had the curiosity to place a mirror before me; and ere long saw re-
> flected there, a curious involved worming and undulation in the
> atmosphere over my head. (Melville 480)

Thus in the spirit of Melville and Bishop's Crusoe, neither "believer nor infidel," I hope my complete faith in all positions put forth here is tempered by a certain healthy doubt. The aim has been to fill a gap in the present dialogue, even at the risk of "talking the life out of the poems."[1]

Perhaps no other mid-twentieth-century North American poet, at present, attracts the attention of so many diverse readers. Although some are unable or unwilling to agree with one another on many questions of ideological and aesthetic import and, more particularly, on which writers best inscribe preferred epistemologies, it seems Bishop is trusted to speak to or for many in their respective tongues. If one were a Classicist, one might argue that this is a sign of her genius: Bishop's "universal" appeal would have nothing to do with chance or the prejudices of the historical moment but rather with her extraordinary talent for remaining relevant to contesting models of the poetic function.

Bishop would have doubted this estimate of her talents, of course. And her humility, the kind that comes through in this 1957 letter to Lowell, is paradoxically appealing at the turn of this confident century:

> And here I must confess (and I imagine most of our contemporaries would confess the same thing), that I am green with envy of your kind of assurance. I feel that I could write in as much detail about my Uncle Artie, say—but what would be the significance? Nothing at all. He became a drunkard, fought with his wife, and spent most of his time fishing—and was ignorant as sin. It is sad; slightly more interesting than having an uncle practicing law in Schenectady maybe, but that's all. Whereas all you have to do is put down the names! And the fact that it seems significant, illustrative, American, etc., gives you, I think, the confidence you display about tackling any idea or theme, *seriously*, in both writing and conversation. In some ways you are the luckiest poet I know!—in some ways not so lucky, either, of course. But it is hell to realize one has wasted half one's talent through timidity that probably could have been overcome if anyone in one's family had had a few grains of sense or education. Well, maybe it's not too late! (*One Art* 351–352)

The poet lacks confidence in her ability to master history, particularly her own. This "timidity," however, translates into a poetics that approaches sociopolitical questions through seemingly haphazard back doors—portals that open suddenly into an alternative heart of "significant, illustrative," and certainly "American" things.

Marianne Boruch is correct in her assessment of Bishop's humor, how "coming into the gravest subjects" it "both unnerves and disarms us" (117). Avoiding the self-righteous inflexibility that is a defining characteristic of much "activist literature," Bishop's verse insists that we never stop questioning our own higher intentions, even as we scrutinize the systems that oppress us or others. And this persistent resistance to fanaticism through humor is one way in which Bishop's poems retain a certain signifying versatility. Because her poems, as Boruch notes, "resist what is predictable, the public 'should' of their circumstances," they do not satisfy a hunger for clean answers or clear enemies (118).

Bishop avoids the "oracular testimonial" rhetoric we tend to expect of post–World War II political poetry—the kind Jarrell sees (and Bishop disapproved of), for example, in the poetry of Muriel Rukseyer whose "real concern," he tells us in *Poetry and the Age*, "is to tell the reader, as excitingly as she can, how he ought to feel about something" (165). Bishop's political poetry—and it *is* political at every lexical turn—tells the reader not what she ought to think or feel about a thing but rather what she might think or feel were she to step beyond the confines of those ordering narratives we fall back on to figure chaos into meaning. Bishop's art may not always refer to specific kinds of oppression; but because it calls our attention to the cultural scripts that predetermine our experience of the world, her "grammar" engages in ethics at its generative core. Bishop's verse is aesthetically activist, as Jacqueline Vaught Brogan argues in her essay "Elizabeth Bishop and a Grammar for the Underclass," because it intrudes on our political understanding of the world.

II

Unusual moments abound in Bishop's best poems as mysteries, like harbingers of hope or despair, suddenly enter—often soundlessly—into the most domestic situations: a moose checks late-night gossip among elderly country people on a bus; African breasts and a half-imagined scream scare a child into adult consciousness in a dentist's waiting room.[2] These fortuitous dramas remind us that nothing must ever be only what it seems. In the poem "Santarém," published in 1979—the year of Bishop's death—we have a similar confounding of the familiar and the strange; and this time, perhaps even more so than in all her other "travel" poems, Bishop persuades us once again that strange is a relative quality. Foreignness is an exception that confirms other rules or realities, be they or be they not our own; and our openness to what is "other" may not only be a supreme source of pleasure, it may also be our salvation.

"Santarém" might be considered one of Bishop's final monuments to the power and necessity of unanticipated, irreducible kinds of beauty. The poem recalls a river and a town high up in the state of Amazonas, a place as exotic to Brazilians as Alaska is to an equal measure of North Americans, especially in the 1950s or 1960s.[3] Yet there is a comfortable familiarity about the poem—a relaxation of poetic form into almost pure and casual prose, perhaps the most proselike of all her poems. Memory has not formalized the vision, nor has age wedged distance between the writer and her subject. Rather, there is a sense that this most removed geographical location and these most foreign cultural circumstances are actually just next door, as potentially familiar as any seaside scene.

Bishop begins the poem by locating herself with language so casual and descriptions so attentive to detail that we are lulled into intimate rapport with what should be a very foreign environment, very exotic activities:

> That golden evening I really wanted to go no farther;
> more than anything else I wanted to stay awhile
> in that conflux of two great rivers, Tapajós, Amazon,
> grandly, silently flowing, flowing east.
> Suddenly there'd been houses, people, and lots of mongrel
> riverboats skittering back and forth
> under a sky of gorgeous, under-lit clouds,
> with everything gilded, burnished along one side,
> and everything bright, cheerful, casual—or so it looked.
> ("Santarém," *The Complete Poems* 185)

She may be remembering it all wrong, she begins by telling us, but what time or the mind may ruin, it may also re-create and in doing so distill thousands of daily impressions into ten or fifteen representative ones. And these are what we live with and share with others like photos of our lives. There is an accumulated lexicon of imagery here that, like memory, weaves old intellectual and tactile experience along with the new: we note that the "gilded, burnished" letters of the big "unlovely" book in "2,000 Illustrations" resurface in the form of "gorgeous, under-lit clouds"; the "awful but cheerful" scene of "The Bight" is now "bright, cheerful, casual." Bishop assumes for us that "Santarém," like Nova Scotia, will offer us information that is necessary because its uses have not been exhausted—even in or perhaps especially in "progressive," postindustrial consciousness.

Things gilded and cheerful continue to circulate in her vocabulary but somehow are less menaced here, more hopeful—in spite of the brief foray into Christian lore and philosophical dualism, the "literary interpretations" that follow and threaten (unsuccessfully) to rationalize the beauty out of the place:

> I liked the place; I liked the idea of the place.
> Two rivers. Hadn't two rivers sprung
> from the Garden of Eden? No, that was four
> and they'd diverged. Here only two

and coming together. Even if one were tempted
to literary interpretations
such as: life/death, right/wrong, male/female
—such notions would have resolved, dissolved, straight off
in that watery, dazzling dialectic. (185)

What dissolves Cartesian thinking also dazzles, and Bishop seems to suggest that places which bring us to the consciousness of less managed, perhaps less manageable, epistemologies also teach us something about beauty. Because this place that teaches also can delight. Although the idea may be patently classical, the medium of instructions here includes "teams of zebus" that are "gentle, proud,"

and *blue,* with down-curved horns and hanging ears (185)

But the fact that they pull carts "with solid wheels" ensures us that these are not sideshows—neither Marianne Moore's circus animals nor Wallace Stevens's wacky baboons. These animals are unexceptional. They live there and work there and dazzle us just the same.

We soon note in the poem just who and what might be considered exotic within the context of the place:

(After the Civil War some Southern Families
came here; here they could still own slaves.
They left occasional blue eyes, English names,
and *oars.* No other place, no one
on all the Amazon's four thousand miles
does anything but paddle.) (186)

The lesson in postcolonialism and race relations is hardly displaced by the oars and hammocks, but it is surely left to us, like strange fruit, to pick up and taste if we are so inclined. Bishop will not insist that we eat unless we choose to. If and when this happens are for us to struggle over. Because we may choose, like Mr. Swan, to dismiss what the Amazon has to offer:

Then—my ship's whistle blew. I couldn't stay.
Back on board, a fellow-passenger, Mr. Swan,
Dutch, the retiring head of Philips Electric,
really a very nice old man,
who wanted to see the Amazon before he died,
asked, "What's that ugly thing?" (187)

It is "back on board" where the only shocking thing in the poem happens. And yet one more elliptical conclusion reverberates throughout yet one more foreign landscape, but this time with the dull thud of a rubber mallet on tin or an ax on wood. The "retiring head of Philips Electric" disappoints us. Yet it is also because of this shortsighted, although economically powerful, tourist that Santarém strikes us as a place we would also wish to see, perhaps turn to for answers to what ails our world's exhausted sense of aesthetics. Mr. Swan's shortsightedness floods the poem with a final, slanted light.

This late poem reminds us that Bishop continued to travel until the end of her life. It also illustrates that she trusted in foreign experience to bring us back to ourselves—if not improved, at least less confident of our desire to order the world according to figures of our own making.

Notes

INTRODUCTION

1. The Brazilian artist Pedro Luiz Correia de Araújo, husband of Bishop's longtime neighbor and confidante Lilli, was instrumental in getting Ouro Prêto listed by UNESCO (Lilli Correia de Araújo, personal interview, Ouro Prêto, Brazil, January 2000).

2. Camille Roman's study on Bishop and politics in the 1950s has appeared since the writing of this text.

CHAPTER 1

1. Longenbach notes, for example, that when Wallace Stevens read *The Waste Land* he "ventured" that "if it is the supreme cry of despair it is Eliot's and not his generation's" (7).

2. Of Eliot and political writing Bishop says,

> Politically I considered myself a socialist, but I disliked "social conscious" writing. I stood up for T. S. Eliot when everybody else was talking about James T. Farrell. The atmosphere at Vassar was left-wing; it was the popular thing. . . . I felt that most of the college girls didn't know much about social conditions. (Bishop in Schwartz and Estess 293)

3. The noun phrase *dazzling dialectic* that concludes the first long stanza in "Santarém" was a favorite of critics in the 1990s. Erkkila concludes her remarkable essay with the suggestion that in reading the "dazzling dialectic" of a politicized Bishop, we can begin to appreciate a similarly complex relation between Modernism and the Left.

4. Two years before her death, Bishop refused to receive McCarthy in her summer home at North Haven because she continued to resent McCarthy's public depiction of her as a lesbian in the character Lakey in *The Group*. She died before receiving this letter in which McCarthy denies the allusion:

> Now that Cal is dead, I feel at liberty to tell you something he told me last summer [of 1977], i.e., that he was convinced you had called off the projected trip to North Haven because you didn't want to see *me*. Because you had got the notion that I had put you and Lota in *The Group*. The character Lakey owed a little something to Margaret Miller but only in her appearance—the

Indian eyes and the dark hair—a kind of hauteur or fine anger maybe or
fathomless scorn. As for the Baroness, I can't remember where I got her if she
came from real life at all. . . . I can see how someone could imagine that you, as
a Vassar contemporary, might be expected to figure in *The Group*. It's perhaps
even strange that you didn't, but that is the fact. I'm highly conscious,
normally, of where the bits and pieces of a book come from—the Baroness
seems to be an exception—and they identify themselves to me by a physical
trait, which may at times be vocal. . . . Well, this is a bore for you, and I won't
say more. But please do believe me. (McCarthy in *One Art* 614)

5. In a 1960 letter to Dr. Baumann, perhaps one of her closest confidants,
Bishop writes:

I have been writing quite a bit of poetry. *The New Yorker* will soon print one
about this house ["Song for the Rainy Season"]. I should be able to get out a
new book next year, I think. I've also, thank heavens, been doing some non–
New Yorker poems, and what I should prefer to do is just sell them an
occasional story and publish poems in other magazines. (*One Art* 391)

6. For examples of this opinion, see Steven Gould Axelrod and Helene Deese,
eds., *Critical Essays on Wallace Stevens* (Boston: G. K. Hall, 1988). See particularly
Fredric Jameson's "Wallace Stevens" in that volume (176–191) in which Jameson
discusses Stevens's appropriation of images of Third World realities, his "disen-
gaged luxury tourist's contemplative contact with ports and maps" (184). See also
Frank Lentricchia's "Versions of Existentialism" in that same volume (98–102);
Charles Doyle, ed., *Wallace Stevens: The Critical Heritage* (Boston: Routledge and Kegan
Paul, 1985); and Marjorie Perloff, "Revolving in Crystal: The Supreme Fiction and
the Impasse of Modernist Lyric," in *Wallace Stevens: The Matrix of Modernism*, ed.
Sanford Schwartz (Princeton: Princeton University Press, 1985), 41–64.

CHAPTER 2

1. Because postcolonial studies is a vast and expanding field, my use of or
reference to terms of that field may strike certain readers, particularly theorists, as
"thin and abstract." Because my intended audience also includes readers outside
postcolonial studies and the book's objectives lie both within and without what I
understand to be the perimeters—however porous—of the field, I have had to
make certain choices.

2. Dickie takes Bishop at her word concerning her political stoicism yet chooses
to ignore Bishop's adamant objection to confessional poetry. Bishop's personal
poetics are once again defined in terms of "strategies of evasion" as Dickie aligns
herself with those same critics and colleagues who profited most from an apolitical
reading of Bishop in the 1940s and 1950s. Editors such as Clement Greenberg of the
Partisan Review admired, for example, what he felt to be the political neutrality of
her poems.

We were too sophisticated to look for anything other than quality. When it
came to politics, of course, we wouldn't publish anything Stalinist or over on

the right, either. Politics were not aesthetic. It was taken for granted that they were separated. (Greenberg in Fountain and Brazeau 93)

The patrician quality of this observation is unsettling for a number of reasons, not the least of which is its fetishizing of the "purely" aesthetic. Like Greenberg, Dickie underestimates the dissolution of binarism in Bishop's poetics, as well as in her life. And also like Greenberg, Dickie must deny one part of the aesthetic-activist equation to promote the other. Dickie's somewhat sustained, close readings of Bishop's language help us admire her conclusions, however, even if we do not accept them because they strike us as earned. Because Erkkila's argument relies more on the strength of its convictions than on the rigor of its textual analysis, she appears to bully the reader with her better conclusions even as Dickie seduces us with her inferior ones.

3. In a 1965 letter to Lowell, Bishop refers to her poem "From Trollope's Journal" as an "anti-Eisenhower" poem, adding, "I think—although it's really almost all Trollope" (One Art 439). This poem has yet to receive much attention from Leftist critics. But in these characteristically tentative remarks, we note that Bishop not only tempers her literary "activism" by distancing her work "from masculine hero-ics," as Palettella terms it; she also suggests that the poem's political import is indistinguishable from its literary subject.

4. Bishop insisted on privacy, and this insistence surely stemmed from a desire to produce within a cultural climate that was potentially hostile to people like her. As her friend and literary coexecutor Frank Bidart notes, "not to be in the closet" for a lesbian during the larger part of her historical period "was to be ghettoized" (Bidart in Fountain and Brazeau 327). Yet at the same time, to come out as Adrienne Rich had—a poet Bishop admired—was to risk becoming a crusader, and Bishop was perhaps even less comfortable with high profile than with exclusion. Bishop spoke approvingly of Auden, one student remembers, considering him "braver" than Allen Ginsberg: "It was obvious Auden was gay, but the notion was that she didn't want to make an issue of these things" (Leithauser in Fountain and Brazeau 329). Yet as more details of Bishop's personal life have been made available to scholars, the more discussions have focused on her addictions and her homosexuality. The fact that she was not as conventional as had been assumed or that the "schoolmarmish" persona she offered the public might say little about the passions fueling the person or the poems appears to be "new" knowledge. The character and artist posing as a "normal woman," in the words of her friend James Merrill, fascinates. Thomas Travisano notes in his 1995 article "The Elizabeth Bishop Phenomenon" that when the "conspiracy of silence" among her friends relaxed after her death in 1979, the reading public "at last" could have "an image capable of sustaining the impression of a major writer"—that is, a figure "vulnerable, fallible, bohemian, lonely, alcoholic, tenacious, ambitious, libidinous, humorous" (920). In spite of the protection of her friends, many of whom are now dead, a veritable feasting on the "sins" of Elizabeth has ensued based on her biography—particularly by Feminists, as C. K. Doreski argues in Elizabeth Bishop: The Restraints of Language.

5. See Fountain and Brazeau, *Remembering Elizabeth Bishop*, 304–307, for discussions of Bishop's uncomfortable relationship with her Harvard colleagues.

CHAPTER 3

1. See "Seascape," "Cootchie," "A Summer's Dream," "At the Fishhouses," "Cape Breton," "The Riverman."

2. The phrase *aesthetic glutton* is borrowed from Bishop herself who used it in 1954 to describe Herbert Read to her friends Ilsa and Kit Barker. Her use of the phrase is more academic, however: "I think Herbert Read is an esthetic glutton— he just has to understand and feel the 'significance' of everything, regardless, and mentally he is an enormous fat man eating away indiscriminately" (*One Art* 290– 291).

CHAPTER 4

1. See again Jameson's critique of Stevens in "Wallace Stevens," 176–191. Where Jameson might well scrutinize Bishop's "contemplative contact with ports and maps," one wonders whether he would also consider the social origins of Bishop's poems repressed in "neutralized" landscapes.

2. The "anthropologist" Clifford Geertz uses the term *ethnographer* to shift emphasis from the study of man to the study of the signs and symbols (*-graphy*) produced by an ethnic group. Similarly, Bishop's poems that register material culture, poems like "Questions of Travel," are concerned with the signs through which a culture presents or represents itself. See Geertz, "From the Native's Point of View: Understanding the Nature of Anthropological Understanding," *Antioch Review* 17, no. 4 (Winter 1957–1958).

CHAPTER 5

1. Lorrie Goldensohn, for example, sees an anguished longing for children on the poet's part. See "The Body's Roses," 70–90.

2. "Crusoe in England" is generally read as a thinly veiled meditation on the loss of Bishop's estranged lover, Lota de Macedo Soares, who died of a sedative overdose (never officially established as accidental or intentional) in New York City on September 25, 1967 (see, for example, McCabe 199; Goldensohn, *Elizabeth Bishop* 67–69; Fountain and Brazeau 265). More recently, the poem has been analyzed for what it reveals about the homosexual nature of Bishop and Soares's relationship or, more important, the covert literary representation of same-sex relationships. Joanne Feit Diehl, for example, sees the poem's Defoe intertext as an enabling blind permitting Bishop to address her personal struggle with public taboo: "In a unisexual and univocal text, Bishop tells a story rich in allusiveness and human suffering while addressing issues of single-sex friendship and the terrors faced by an intense subjectivity that seeks expression in stark isolation" (91–110). To look at the political and sociological ramifications of tabooed kinds of love engages the personal at its most politically vulnerable level. Limiting this poem's ambitious transhistorical objectives to this alone tends, however, to reconfirm

previous—albeit enhanced—autobiographical readings. Bishop was horrified by the suggestion that "Crusoe in England" was an autobiographical metaphor for Brazil and Lota (Frank Bidart in Fountain and Brazeau 333). And it is interesting that in spite of efforts to steer Bishop's poems toward historically, socially, or politically engaged interpretations, it is still the poet herself who insists the most ardently against an autotelic reading of her texts.

CONCLUSION

1. Although Bishop's poetry and prose impel readers to lose faith in their paradigms, her own reservations about the indulgences of close textual analysis put appropriate pressure on the pages at hand:

> The analysis of poetry is growing more and more pretentious and deadly. After a session with a few of the highbrow magazines one doesn't want to look at a poem for weeks, much less start writing one. The situation is reminiscent of those places along the coast where warnings are posted telling one not to walk too near the edge of the cliffs because they have been undermined by the sea and may collapse at any minute.
>
> This does not mean I am opposed to all close analysis and criticism. But I am opposed to making poetry monstrous or boring and proceeding to talk the very life out of it. (Bishop in Schwartz and Estess 281)

Any attempt to breathe too much political life into the syntactic choices in the poems also risks collapsing the poems into allegorical representations. Readings that attempt to isolate the poems' linguistic resistance to cultural hegemony, for example, may fashion the texts into imaginary cliffs by gleaning from them "monstrous" messages about the evils of modern, "First World" culture. And counterarguments about the corrective wisdom of the poet may prove "boring." Such are the immediate dangers of the present argument.

2. See Helen Vendler's early discussion of Freud's "unheimlich," or the uncanny, and Bishop's poems in "Domestication, Domesticity, and the Otherworldly," 32–48.

3. The construction of the Transamazonica highway in the early 1970s has since made travel to and within northern Brazil less formidable. Although this enormous and expensive initiative has brought "civilization" to many backwater areas in Amazonia, including Santarém, the devastating effects on the environment and local populations are difficult to "figure." It is known that by 1989, 10 percent of the Amazon forest had been destroyed to make way for this highway system—a project backed and managed in great part by the World Bank, the International Monetary Fund, other international banks, and the United States.

Works Cited

Ashbery, John. "Rev. of *The Complete Poems*, by Elizabeth Bishop." *New York Times Book Review* (June 1, 1969): 8.

Auden, W. H. *The Dyer's Hand*. New York: Vintage International, 1989.

Beerbohm, Max. "Last Acts." In his *Around Theaters*. New York: Simon and Schuster, 1954.

Bell, Pearl. "Dona Elizabetchy." *Partisan Review* 58 (1991): 28–52.

Bhabha, Homi. *The Location of Culture*. New York: Routledge, 1994.

Bishop, Elizabeth. *Brazil*. New York: Time Incorporated, 1962.

———. *The Collected Prose*. Ed. Robert Giroux. New York: Farrar, Straus and Giroux, 1984.

———. *The Complete Poems*. New York: Farrar, Straus and Giroux, 1983.

———. "Dimensions for a Novel." *Vassar Journal of Undergraduate Studies* 8 (May 1935): 95–103.

———. *One Art: Elizabeth Bishop Letters*. Ed. Robert Giroux. New York: Noonday, 1994.

———. *Questions of Travel*. New York: Farrar, Straus and Giroux, 1965.

Blanton, Casey. *Travel Writing: The Self and the World*. New York: Twayne, 1997.

Bohls, Elizabeth. *Women Travel Writers and the Language of Aesthetics 1716–1808*. Cambridge: Cambridge University Press, 1995.

Boruch, Marianne. "From Bishop's Blue Pharmacy." *New England Review* 13 (1990): 112–120.

Brogan, Jacqueline Vaught. "Elizabeth Bishop and a Grammar for the Underclass: Response to Jonathan Ausubel's 'Subjected People.'" *Connotations* 4, nos. 1–2 (1994–1995): 83–97.

Crane, Hart. "Chaplinesque." In *Anthology of American Literature*. Ed. George McMichael. New York: Macmillan, 1985.

Defoe, Daniel. *Robinson Crusoe*. New York: Bantam, 1981.

Dickie, Margaret. "Elizabeth Bishop: Text and Subtext." *Southern Atlantic Review* 59 (1994): 1–19.

Diehl, Joanne Feit. *Women Poets and the American Sublime*. Bloomington: Indiana University Press, 1990.

Doreski, C. K. *Elizabeth Bishop: The Restraints of Language*. New York: Oxford University Press, 1993.

Eagleton, Terry. *The Ideology of the Aesthetic*. Cambridge: Basil Blackwell, 1990.

Erkkila, Betsy. "Elizabeth Bishop, Modernism, and the Left." *American Literary History* 8 (1996): 284–310.

Fountain, Gary, and Peter Brazeau. *Remembering Elizabeth Bishop: An Oral Biography.* Amherst: University of Massachusetts Press, 1994.

Fussell, Paul. *Abroad: British Literary Travel Between the Wars.* New York: Oxford University Press, 1980.

Genette, Gerard. *Narrative Discourse.* Ithaca: Cornell University Press, 1980.

Goldensohn, Lorrie. "The Body's Roses." In *The Geography of Gender.* Ed. Marilyn May Lombardi. Charlottesville: University Press of Virginia, 1993.

———. *Elizabeth Bishop: The Biography of a Poetry.* New York: Columbia University Press, 1992.

Gregory, Horace. "Introduction." In *New Letters in America.* New York: W. W. Norton, 1937.

Harrison, Victoria. "Recording a Life." In *Geography of Gender.* Ed. Marilyn Lombardi. Charlottesville: University Press of Virginia, 1993.

Heat-Moon, William Least. "Journeys into Kansas." In *Temperamental Journeys: Essays on the Modern Literature of Travel.* Ed. Michael Kowalenski. Athens: University of Georgia Press, 1992.

Homer. *The Odyssey.* Middlesex: Penguin, 1946.

Jameson, Fredric. "Wallace Stevens." In *Critical Essays on Wallace Stevens.* Eds. Steven Gould Axelrod and Helen Deese. Boston: G. K. Hall, 1988.

Jarrell, Randall. *Poetry and the Age.* New York: Ecco, 1953.

Kalstone, David. *Becoming a Poet: Elizabeth Bishop with Marianne Moore and Robert Lowell.* New York: Farrar, Straus and Giroux, 1989.

———. *Five Temperaments.* New York: Oxford University Press, 1977.

Kaplan, Caren. *Questions of Travel.* Durham: Duke University Press, 1996.

Longenbach, James. *Modern Poetry After Modernism.* New York: Oxford University Press, 1997.

Matos, Jacinta. "Old Journeys Revisited: Aspects of Postwar English Travel Writing." In *Temperamental Journeys: Essays on the Modern Literature of Travel.* Ed. Michael Kowalenski. Athens: University of Georgia Press, 1992.

McCabe, Susan. *Elizabeth Bishop: Her Poetics of Loss.* University Park: Pennsylvania State University Press, 1994.

McCarthy, Mary. *The Group.* New York: Signet, 1954.

Melville, Herman. *Moby Dick.* New York: Macmillan, 1964.

Monteiro, George. *Conversations with Elizabeth Bishop.* Jackson: University of Mississippi Press, 1996.

Palettella, John. "'That Sense of Constant Re-adjustment': The Great Depression and the Provisional Politics of Elizabeth Bishop's *North and South.*" *Contemporary Literature* 31, no. 1 (1993): 18–43.

Pascal, Blaise. *Pensées.* Paris: Bordas, 1966.

Phillips, Richard. *Mapping Men and Empire.* New York: Routledge, 1997.

Riffaterre, Michael. *Fictional Truth.* Baltimore: Johns Hopkins University Press, 1990.

Schwartz, Lloyd, and Sybil P. Estess. *Elizabeth Bishop and Her Art.* Ann Arbor: University of Michigan Press, 1983.

Shetley, Vernon. *After the Death of Poetry*. Durham: Duke University Press, 1993.

Stevens, Wallace. *The Collected Poems*. New York: Vintage, 1990.

———. *The Necessary Angel*. New York: Vintage, 1951.

Travisano, Thomas. "The Elizabeth Bishop Phenomenon." *New Literary History* 26 (1995): 903–930.

van Gogh, Vincent. *The Letters of Vincent van Gogh*. Ed. Mark Roskill. New York: Atheneum, 1979.

Vendler, Helen. "Domestication, Domesticity, and the Otherworldly." In *Elizabeth Bishop and Her Art*. Eds. Lloyd Schwartz and Sybil P. Estess. Ann Arbor: University of Michigan Press, 1983.

Von Hallberg, Robert. "Tourism and Postwar Poetry." In *Temperamental Journeys: Essays on the Modern Literature of Travel*. Ed. Michael Kowalenski. Athens: University of Georgia Press, 1992.

Index